BEST [

CLASSIC EX

C000235912

A DRAGON?

No-one knows exactly how the *dragon tree (drago)* – actually a lily which can live for 1,000 years – got its name, but its lush crown has become a symbol of Tenerife. The most beautiful specimen is in Icod de los Vinos.

➤ p. 54, The Northwest & Teide National Park

GAZE INTO INFINITY

The *Observatorio del Teide* (photo) is the island's super-modern observatory. Tenerife's consistently clear weather makes for great stargazing.

➤ p. 64, The Northwest & Teide National Park

MONUMENTAL PYRAMIDS

The pyramids at *Güimar* suggest that the Canaries were used as a stopping point between the Old and New Worlds long before Columbus, although that theory is disputed …

➤ p. 91, The Southeast

PINE TREES THAT MILK THE CLOUDS

The exceptionally long needles on the Canarian pine means it can "milk" moisture from the clouds while its thick bark protects it from forest fires. One particularly fine example is the *Pino Gordo*.

➤ p. 97, The Southeast

EAT LIKE A GUANCHE

Gofio, a finely ground roasted grain, was the ultimate staple of the Guanche (early island settlers). For a long time it was derided as "poor people's food" but is now making a comeback as an element of modern Canarian cuisine. You can even get *gofio* mousse at restaurants like *El Gomero*.

➤ p. 108, The Southwest

GET TO KNOW TENERIFE

Water-based fun at Lago Martiánez in Puerto de la Cruz

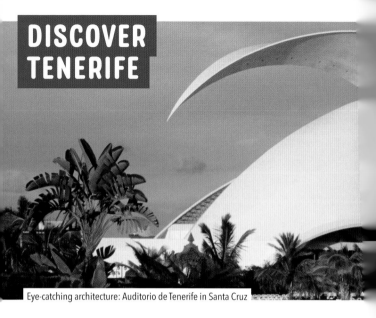

DISCOVER TENERIFE

Eye-catching architecture: Auditorio de Tenerife in Santa Cruz

A mountain full of mystery. Planes circle the Pico del Teide at a respectful distance, before beginning their descent to Tenerife. Visible from miles away, it acts as a signpost and a symbol for the island. Dense cloud cover often separates it from the world below. The king of all volcanoes, it surveys the hostile lunar landscape below from a great height. It's an impressive sight, but for our forebears it was greatly feared. There was an eruption on its northern slopes as recently as 1909.

WRATH OF A GOD
Ancient legends reported the existence of an island called Nivaria, or "snowy one". The Guanche, Tenerife's first settlers, feared that an angry god, Guayote, was orchestrating Teide's eruptions, and Columbus saw the sparks and smoke as a

5th century BCE
Settlement by North African Berbers

1496
Alonso Fernández de Lugo conquers Tenerife

16th century
The Canary Islands become Spain's first colony

1706
A volcanic eruption largely destroys the town of Garachico

1852
The Canary Islands become a free trade zone and, as a result, British influence grows

Late 19th century
The cultivation and export of bananas brings economic prosperity to Tenerife

bad omen for his voyage of discovery. In 1799, Alexander von Humboldt was struck by the fact that at daybreak the first rays of sunshine illuminated the summit, while on the coast darkness still reigned: the Canarian day begins and ends on Mount Teide (3,718m), Spain's highest mountain.

A BIT OF EVERYTHING

At 2,034km² Tenerife is the largest of the seven "Islands of Eternal Spring", as the Canaries were known in ancient Greece. Its diversity is what makes Tenerife so fascinating: blue ocean, great beaches, rugged cliffs and gorges, dense forests, barren wastelands and Mount Teide rising out of a bizarre sea of rock. Culturally it has a lot to offer too in its colonial towns, museums and churches. You can sit with the locals in down-to-earth bars, enjoy traditional food, drink their strong wines and share in lively festivals. Surf, dive, hike, cycle, turn night into day or simply lie back and relax – there is no place for boredom on Tenerife. And the sun shines throughout the year.

ELYSIAN WINDS

Arriving at Reina Sofía airport can be something of a shock: barren urban sprawl as far as the eye can see and a parched landscape – water is a rare and precious commodity here. But don't worry, only the southeast is quite this inhospitable. No surprise then that Tenerife's residents have always preferred La Laguna's plateau and the Valle de la Orotava – the island's greenest spot. Northeastern trade winds are responsible for the conditions here, bringing moist air to the north at

1936-39
The Spanish Civil War – which began on the Canary Islands – ushers in Franco's dictatorship

From 1960
Charter flights bring tourists to the islands in large numbers

1975
After Franco's death, Spain becomes a parliamentary monarchy

1986
Spain joins the EU and NATO

2009-17
The global financial crisis causes many to lose their jobs and homes

2018
Tourism booms on the "safe" Canary Islands

altitudes of 700–1,700m. This air collects in the island's mountainous centre and forms clouds which provide not only rain but much-needed shade, making the area cooler and greener. If you are worried about Saharan temperatures (the west coast of Africa is only 300km away, after all), you will be pleasantly surprised. The climate here is more like a permanent spring – it never gets much hotter than 30°C in summer or cooler than 20°C degrees in winter.

GET INVOLVED IN TENERIFE LIFE!

If you want to get to know the island and its people, you need to explore the Zona metropolitana, which includes both the old and new capitals. Almost one-third of the 800,000 Tinerfeños live in the La Laguna and Santa Cruz area. In recent years the historic centre of La Laguna has been restored and is now free of traffic and has UNESCO World Heritage Site status. In Santa Cruz, internationally renowned architects have designed grand new buildings, such as the Auditorium, the Congress Hall and the TEA arts centre. Ambitious plans for the future include a facelift for the seafront as far as the beach in San Andrés, 10km away, although most of these projects have fallen victim to the global financial crisis.

EVERYTHING WILL BE OK!

The Canaries have been "war profiteers" for years, with many holidaymakers that used to travel to North Africa or the Middle East now opting for the archipelago. Still the stampede of tourists has barely managed to lower the unemployment rate (20 per cent in 2020). Instead of hiring new staff, hotel owners are increasing the workload of their existing employees. But visitors will hardly notice the impact on everyday life as, despite everything, the islanders stay cheerful and keep celebrating at boisterous festivals, calling in at their favourite cafés and bars, and taking a siesta between 1pm and 5pm every day. Unlike their ancestors, few today consider emigration.

AT A GLANCE

925,595
Inhabitants on the island

Birmingham: 1,149,000

350km
Coastline

Welsh coastline: 1,400km

2,034km²
Surface area

Isle of Wight: 381km²

**HIGHEST MOUNTAIN:
TEIDE**

3,718m
Peak only accessible
with a permit

**SNOW IS POSSIBLE
ON TENERIFE ABOVE
2,000M**

**AVERAGE LIFE
EXPECTANCY:**

**82.7
years**

In the UK:
81.6 years

THE AFRICAN CONTINENT IS 288KM AWAY

The Spanish mainland is 1,274km away

SANTA CRUZ

Largest city with 204,000 inhabitants
(360,000 incl. La Laguna)
Sunderland has 344,000 inhabitants

**THE CARNIVAL
QUEEN'S COSTUME**
costs more then
20,000 euros

420 LITRES OF WATER
are needed to harvest
1kg of bananas

UNDERSTAND TENERIFE

DRAGONS & RED, RED FLOWERS

No plant has captured the imagination of the Canary islanders quite like the dragon tree, which became extinct except on the Macaronesian islands (Canaries, Madeira, Azores, Cape Verde) 20 million years ago, although close relatives do exist in Africa and Asia. The Guanches regarded the tree as sacred, largely because of its resin, known as "dragon's blood", which turns dark red when exposed to the air and which was once used in the preparation of medicinal treatments. If you cut a branch from the *drago*, it grows back as quickly as "the head of a dragon". That is why early naturalists gave the tree its fairytale-inspired botanical name *Dracaena drago*. The locals still revere their dragon trees – there's hardly a garden in the Canary Islands without one.

The Tenerife bugloss *(Echium wildpretii)* is another wonderful plant. Its botanical name refers to the Swiss botanist Hermann Wildpret, but it's a true Tinerfeño. It has a 2-m-high flower head that rises upwards like a viper

Dragon trees grow up to 20m tall

enchanted by a snake charmer and is studded with thousands of small, glowing red flowers – no bee (or person) can miss it when it is in flower from May to June. The Tenerife bugloss is hardy and grows well above the treeline – a bright exclamation mark in a volcanic landscape. Close relatives of the Tenerife bugloss grow at lower elevations, but they are smaller and their blossoms are blue or white.

MYSTERIOUS GUANCHES

Little is known about the island's original inhabitants, whose name roughly means "sons of Tenerife". The Guanches colonised the archipelago from the fifth century BCE, arriving in several waves, and it is thought they were descended from the Berbers of North Africa. They were primarily farmers who reared goats and sheep and were ruled by a *mencey* (type of king). When the Spanish settlers arrived on the Canaries, the nine sons of the Mencey Bezenuria were in power. Larger-than-life bronze statues of them line the waterfront promenade of Plaza Patrona de Canarias in Candelaria. The Guanches mostly lived in caves, where they buried their mummified dead.

After Europeans subjugated the native people, the surviving population was quickly integrated into the population of the conquerors. Their legacy can be seen in the *Museo del Hombre y la Naturaleza* in Santa Cruz, in *the Museo Arqueológico* in Puerto de la Cruz, and also at the mysterious *Pirámides de Güímar*.

COLOURFUL CARNIVALS

Months of preparation are needed for Tenerife's exuberant *Carnaval* and the wild weeks in February and March. *Carrozas* or floats have to be built and decorated, costumes sewn and masks carefully crafted. *Murgas* or troupes of jesters, compete with one another to make the best outfits, to sing the cheekiest songs and to play the weirdest music. During the *desfiles* (processions) they dance and frolic noisily through the streets. In Santa Cruz de Tenerife huge seas of wildly celebrating bodies pack every corner of the city.

Each night after these parades, which are transmitted live on national Spanish television, there is a *mogollón*, when Tinerfeños dance to Latin beats until the early hours of the morning. And it goes on for days and weeks.

The official climax is the election of the Reina del Carnaval. It is not beauty that determines who is crowned carnival queen, but the grace with which she manages to carry the extremely heavy and extravagant costume — itself worth as much as a mid-range car.

The grand finale of *Carnaval* is the *Entierro de la Sardina*, the burial of the sardine. Once again there is a spectacular, colourful parade, but this time a huge cardboard sardine is dragged through the streets. It ends with a pyrotechnic explosion of Roman candles, rockets and firecrackers. Santa Cruz's Casa del Carnaval allows you to soak up the carnival vibes all year round. (See p. 73)

INSIDER TIP

Missed the carnival? Never mind!

THE MUSIC OF FORTUNE

Barrios Orquestrados is a project that has made its way to the Canary Islands from Venezuela. Children and teenagers from troubled areas, far removed from grand concert halls and conservatoires, learn from professional musicians and have weekly choir sessions with their parents. The idea is to show that creativity and opportunity can help keep young people away from violence.

MADONNA OF THE SEA

A lot of fuss over one tiny statue. A town is named after her, huge events are organised in her honour and taxi drivers display pictures of her in their cars. The *Virgen de Candelaria* is the crowned queen of Tenerife and has been the island's patron saint for over 500 years. Her career began in the early 15th century when a few Guanches found a Gothic statue of the Madonna and Child, which had been washed ashore near Candelaria. Legend has it that the fearful shepherds wanted to throw stones at it, but their arms became paralysed mid-lob. Impressed by the figure's apparent magical powers, the indigenous Canarians transported the figure into a cave and began to worship it.

When Catholic missionaries arrived on the island, it was easy for them to use this belief to convert the Guanches to the faith of that "magical woman". The statue was given the

No outfit is too colourful for a Canarian Carnival

name Our Lady of Candelaria and a small church was built there in her honour. However, in 1826, a freak wave washed the church and the Madonna out to sea. Today's statue was made in 1827 by a local artist and, of course, a new church was built soon after. (See p. 90)

SHADY HOUSES

You may be surprised to see that many elaborately crafted wooden doors and windows are locked up and shuttered and that not a soul can be seen on the splendidly carved balconies. Where the sun beats down all year round, people are more likely to seek shelter in the shade. Closely latticed shutters allow the air to circulate, but they also block the sun, creating an air-conditioning effect.

The façades are gleaming white to reflect the sunlight while exposed stone, door and window frames cut from blocks of rough volcanic stone and pale red roof tiles provide strong contrasts. The hub of a house is the patio, the inner courtyard, which provides access to all the rooms through arcades on each floor. They will often have beautiful plants and there might even be a fountain to create a cool, green retreat from the heat.

Churches and town houses have carved and brightly painted timber ceilings inside – often in the Moorish-inspired Mudéjar style. La Orotava and La Laguna showcase lovely examples of Canarian architecture. The best-preserved mountain village in Tenerife is Masca, where the houses are dry stone walled – that is, they use no mortar.

TRUE OR FALSE?

365 DAYS OF SUN A YEAR?

False! There is a very good chance of seeing a sign on the way to Teide directing you to a diversion because the road is *Cortada por nieve* (closed due to snow). It snows across the island at altitudes above 2,000m and the whole of the north is often enveloped in cloud. However, the south does get more than 300 days of sun a year.

VOLCANOS ARE DANGEROUS?

True! The last eruption on Tenerife was in 1909 and geologists think another is due but have no idea if it will be in 1,000, 100 or 2 years. Every spasm on the volcanoes is measured to check if evacuation is needed. The volcano on El Hierro, Tenerife's sister island, was kind enough to announce its eruption with a series of quakes in 2011/12.

Take the cable car up to the wintery world of Teide National Park

EQUATORIAL ICE

It's only 300km to the Sahara Desert – so can it really snow here? It can, and it does. Teide National Park lies at an elevation of over 2,000m – with the mountain itself reaching 3,718m – and temperatures can dip below freezing there. When it does snow, Canary Islanders will make the trek to the top in order to enjoy the white stuff.

Snow and ice played an important commercial role on Tenerife at the time of the Spanish conquest. A new occupation, that of ice vendors or *neveros*, emerged. They earned a living from first making the dangerous multi-day ascent to the top of Teide, then transporting their cold cargo, either on donkeys or on their backs, down into the villages and selling it.

SOS H$_2$O

The downside of a place where the sun always shines is a shortage of water. Once upon a time there were many rivers on Tenerife and the dense pine and laurel forests absorbed the moisture from the trade winds. Wells and shafts stretching for kilometres, known as galleries, were driven deep into the mountains, reaching underground water supplies, which kept the farmers' crops irrigated. But since then, most of the trees have been felled and many of the wells have run

only uses about 10 per cent of the water with agriculture taking the lion's share, about 70 per cent. Please set a good example and don't waste water.

PUTTING THE CANARY INTO THE CANARY ISLANDS

Its plumage is yellow, its song melodic. Many people are familiar with the canary, but they may not know that it is also the name of an archipelago in the Atlantic.

The domestic canary is a relative of the wild *Serenus canaria*, a bird which still inhabits the forests of the archipelago. It also sings beautifully, but its appearance is not so spectacular which is why the canary we know today was selectively bred until it acquired its current form.

DON'T GET HURT!

Lucha canaria, Canarian wrestling, dates from the time of the Guanches. Twelve contestants in two teams compete in pairs against each other in a sand-lined ring about 15m in diameter. In a clearly defined starting position they lean forward face-to-face and attempt to grab the rolled-up trouser leg of the opponent with their left hand. During the match, which lasts a maximum of three minutes, the *luchadores* must try, using different grips, to throw their opponent to the ground. If you floor your opponent twice, you win. The team with the most victories wins the contest. If you would like to watch a match, enquire at the tourist information office about fixtures; every major town has its own arena *(terrero de lucha canaria)*.

dry. Rainwater is collected in a few reservoirs but it is mainly seawater desalination plants that supply the holiday resorts of Tenerife, whose nine golf courses need huge quantities of water.

This requires money and energy; the latter is being generated mainly through the environmentally harmful burning of oil. Newer systems are being developed using a more environmentally friendly osmosis procedure, whereby the salt is mechanically removed from the seawater. It is forced through a semi-permeable membrane, which lets through the water molecules, but blocks the larger salt particles. Tourism

EATING
SHOPPING
SPORT

Stroll around to your heart's content in Santa Cruz de Tenerife

EATING & DRINKING

Gofio, *mojo* and *bienmesabe*: international fast food is a thing of the past. Make sure you try Tenerife's traditional cuisine.

GO GOFIO

For millennia, the Canary Islands' staple has been *gofio*, a flour made of roasted maize, millet or barley. The grain was cultivated on terraces constructed in the mountains. Wherever water gushed through gorges, millstones ground flour. This yellow or light brown powder is a filling and very versatile protein-rich food. In addition, it combines excellently with a wide variety of flavours. If you see *gofio escaldado*, a *caldo* (broth) made with thickened *gofio* flour, give it a go. It's served the traditional way with raw red onion slices. Today innovative chefs even mix finely ground ⚑ *gofio* with ice cream and banana purée – for daring, but very tasty creations.

A BOWL OF SOUP, SIR?

Soups and stews are very popular. Freshly prepared *sopas* are served at almost every restaurant that specialises in local cuisine. One particularly good speciality is *potaje canario*, a hearty vegetable soup.

If you think cress is only good for egg sandwiches, then you must try cress soup! This classic dish is made using large-leaved wild cress which is spicier than its farmed cousin. Traditionally *potaje de berros* is served in a wooden bowl and garnished with half a corn on the cob.

INSIDER TIP
Eat like the locals

PICKLES & PRESERVES

For Tinerfeños survival has always depended on the optimum use of their resources. They tended sheep and goats and later began to hunt rabbits. But meat and fish remained a

Cress soup served with *papas arrugadas* (left), traditional *gofio* bread and cheese (right)

luxury that, until the 20th century, few islanders could afford.

Food had to be dried or preserved in salt to stop it going off, so the islanders developed a speciality known as *adobos*. Food was pickled for weeks, sometimes months, in hot sauces made from oil, vinegar, bay leaf, herbs, garlic and pepper; only then did its typical flavour develop.

LIFE WITHOUT LEFTOVERS

Leftovers as we understand them today did not exist in the past. Anything left uneaten went into stews with names like *ropa vieja* (old clothes) – an appetising reference to its recycled contents. Today, *ropa vieja*, *puchero* and *rancho canario*, meat and vegetable stews, are freshly prepared with pork, chickpeas, potatoes, pasta, onions, saffron, garlic and spicy chorizo. These are among the tastiest

– and most traditional – dishes Tenerife has to offer.

Ingredients from every corner of the globe have been incorporated into the local cuisine: fennel from Andalusia, yams from Africa, saffron from La Mancha, and chayote from Venezuela. A good reminder that for 400 years the Canary Islands were the meeting point of three continents.

WRINKLY POTATOES...

The most traditional side dish is *papas arrugadas*. The famous "wrinkly potatoes", much-loved by tourists, are served in every restaurant. They are a special variety: small, dark on the outside, yellow inside. The potatoes are normally accompanied by *mojo*, a red or green spicy sauce.

FISH – GRILLED ON A PLATE

Seafood is, of course, on every menu in Tenerife. Normally grilled on a hot

Finally, every meal is rounded off with a *cortado* or a *solo* — an espresso with or without milk.

GOOD ACCOMPANIMENTS

Locals will drink Tenerife's dry lager, Dorada, or a bottle of the island's wine with their food. Tenerife is the biggest wine producer in the Canary Islands. Cultivation started shortly after the Conquista and, before long, many barrels were being exported back to Europe. But the colonial rivalry between Spain and England destroyed what was a thriving trade.

Vine diseases caused further damage to the island's wine industry. The tide turned only after Spain joined the EU; money from Brussels was invested in agriculture and the Tinerfeños began to rediscover their local tipples. Family wineries were modernised, new bodegas were opened and before long wines from Tenerife were winning international prizes.

Today on Tenerife there are five *Denominaciones de Origen* (Protected Designation of Origin). Grapes are harvested in September, so that young wine can be drunk by early November – when wine festivals take place in Icod de los Vinos, Puerto de la Cruz and Tacoronte. The best place to taste the island's vintages is the Casa del Vino (see p. 82) in El Sauzal. Tastings are cheap and generous!

Tenerife's wine – both red and white – is well worth trying

metal plate *a la plancha*, the tastiest options include *cherne*, *sama*, *caballa* and *bocinegro*. All of these are local fish and, once lightly grilled and served with salad and *mojo*, the depth of their flavour is revealed. Two types of octopus, *pulpo* and *choco*, are also extremely popular.

FABULOUS FINALE

Every meal needs a good ending. A huge variety of fruit, from apricots to mangos and guavas, is grown on the Canary Islands. These are often served with the ubiquitous *flan* or set custard.

However, the best Canarian dessert has to be *bienmesabe*, a blend of honey, lime or lemon, almonds and eggs.

Today's Menu

Starters

CALDO DE PESCADO
Fish soup with potatoes and herbs

POTAJE CANARIO
Chickpea, potato and vegetable soup

POTAJE DE BERROS
Cress stew with squash, potatoes
and sweetcorn

Mains

CHERNE AL CILANTRO
Sea bream in a coriander sauce

SANCOCHO CANARIO
Saltfish stew with vegetables and
sweet potato.

CONEJO AL SALMOREJO
Pan-fried rabbit, marinated in bay
leaves, garlic and wine

**CARNE DE CABRA/
BAIFO EN ADOBO**
Goat in a peppery sauce

Side dishes

MOJO ROJO
Spicy chilli sauce with oil, garlic, vinegar
and salt

MOJO VERDE
A milder version with coriander

PAPAS ARRUGADAS
Potatoes boiled in brine whose skin has
begun to wrinkle (*arrugado* in Spanish)

GOFIO ESCALDADO
Roasted grain flour mixed with fish
stock to form a paste

Desserts

LECHE ASADA
A custard made of eggs, lemon zest,
cinnamon and sugar

BIENMESABE
A thick dessert made with honey,
almonds, egg yolks and lemons
(its name means "this is tasty")

FLAN CASERO
A home-made set custard

SHOPPING

From shopping outlets to luxury boutiques and farmers' markets – Tinerfeños love to shop and there's plenty on offer.

LOCAL FAVOURITES

Tinerfeños shop in Santa Cruz, which not only has the huge *El Corte Inglés* department store but also a range of smaller boutiques. In the old town, *Calle del Castillo* is home to a variety of global brands from Desigual to Zara. The smaller streets leading off it have some more interesting, less internationally recognisable shops. The market, *Mercado Nuestra Señora de África*, is piled high with fruit and there is a flea market *(rastro)* around it on Sundays.

For food and drink – and a great atmosphere – the farmers' markets *(mercadillos de agricultor)* are the best choice. These are held at weekends in places like Tacoronte, where local farmers, beekeepers and winemakers come to sell their wares.

BLOOMING GREAT SOUVENIRS

One delightful souvenir is the exotic bird of paradise plant *(strelitzia)*, which grows on Tenerife. You can even buy it at the airport shop after check-in. As an alternative, you can purchase a bag of *drago* seeds and plant dragon trees at home!

WHEEL OF TIME

Alfarería – bowls, plates, jugs and drinking vessels – were essential basic commodities for everyday life in the past. Today it is their simplicity that gives them their special appeal. In the village of Arguayo, near Santiago del Teide, pottery is still made using traditional methods. Without using a wheel, the potters coil the clay and the

Feast your eyes and palate: *mojo sauce* (left) and *strelitzie* or bird of paradise flower (right)

natural umber, rust red or black of the vessels is left unpainted.

Arguayo is not the only place selling ceramics; there is also a chain of state-run shops, Artenerife *(artenerife. com)*, which ensures that makers get a fair price. They have shops in Santa Cruz, La Orotaya, Playa de las Américas and Los Cristianos.

HEIGHT OF FASHION

Gran Canaria is home to the Moda Cálida brand and, not wanting to be left behind, Tenerife now has a label of its own: Tenerife Moda, whose designers are supported by the island's government. Some have made it onto the international stage, such as *Noemi Felipe*'s Sexy Beach Wear, *Roselinde*'s bold and cheeky accessories *(roselinde.net)* and By Loleiro's unusual hats *(byloleiro.com)*.

Events are organised to promote the brand, the most famous of which is the *Feria de la Moda* in April *(tenerife moda.com)*.

There's also an online magazine which focuses on the island's hottest trends *(short.travel/ten5)*.

INCREDIBLE MEMORIES

Many people think food is the best souvenir. And the Canary Islands offer a great selection including world-class cheese from happy goats, the delicious *bienmesabe* almond dessert, liqueurs made from palm juice or bananas and locally made cakes. *Gofio* (see p. 26) can be bought in every supermarket or directly from one of Tenerife's last working flour mills in La Orotava.

SPORT & ACTIVITIES

With trade winds from the northeast sweeping along Tenerife's coasts, it is no surprise that windsurfing is the most popular water sport on the island. Bodyboarding off Playa de las Américas and Puerto de la Cruz has become very popular too.

There are also plenty of land-based activities – from trail running to hiking, biking, climbing, paragliding and golf… Agencies in the resort towns rent equipment and offer courses at all levels.

When it is cold in northern Europe, lots of pro sportspeople come to Tenerife to train. If you want to join them, the *T3 Athletic Sphere (daily 8am–10pm | La Caleta | Av. de los Acantillados s/n | tel. 922 78 27 55 | tenerifetoptraining.com)*, high above La Caleta/Costa Adeje, has facilities for almost any sport you care to think of, from beach volleyball to swimming (the Olympic-size pool has underwater cameras to help you analyse your performance). And there's a luxurious spa for relaxing.

The island's biggest sporting event, the *Vuelta Ciclista* – round-the-island cycle race – takes place in September.

CLIMBING PARK

At *Forestal Park Tenerife (admission 22 euros, children up to 12 17 euros | El Rosario | forestalparktenerife.es)*, a ropes course in a pine forest in the island's north, you can test your climbing skills. Ziplines up to 200m long and platforms 30m up in the air will give you a real rush.

CYCLING

Tenerife has become very popular among professional road racers because of its steep roads and the mild winter climate. However, amateurs will find flat roads by the coast

Mountain bikers will have a great time on Tenerife's trails

(although they will have to put up with a lot of traffic). Please note: Helmets are compulsory for cyclists in Spain. Mountain-bikers are allowed to go off-road.

If you're in a holiday resort, hiring a bike for a day will cost from 16 euros, for a week from 95 euros. Guided bike tours start at 40 euros plus bike hire. *Bike Point (bikepointtenerife.com)* is a good supplier with locations in El Médano and Playa de las Américas.

DIVING
Many diving schools offer courses and trips to some amazing underwater sites – not too far from the coast. Snorkelers exploring the inshore waters will catch a glimpse of a few small fish, but scuba divers will be able to see barracudas, parrot fish, mantas, tuna and, if they're lucky, whales and dolphins. Solo diving is forbidden.

The *Centro de Buceo Atlantik (tel. 922 36 2801 | tenerife-buceo.com)* in Puerto de la Cruz runs dives from 38 euros; beginner courses start at 75 euros. In Playa de las Américas, the *Aqua-Marina Dive Centre (Av. Arquitecto Gómez Cuesta 12 | tel. 651 16 37 07 | aquamarinadivingtenerife. com)* is recommended. In Playa Paraíso, *Dive Center Aquanautic (tel. 922 74 18 81 | tauchen-auf-teneriffa. com)* offers a wide range of tours, as does *Divería (Plaza 12 | tel. 603 76 27 54 | diveria.net)* in Alcalá.

GOLF
Golfers can tee off year round on three 27-hole, four 18-hole and two 9-hole golf courses. All charge a green fee but are open to the public (details are under Sport & activities in the regional chapters).

PARAGLIDING

Float above volcanoes and come down to land on white sands. A pro will be strapped to you while you fly like a bird above mountains and valleys.

INSIDER TIP
The ultimate thrill

There are no fewer than 40 take-off points on the island. The best one, *Izaña*, is on the Cumbre Dorsal near the observatory, at a height of 2,350m. Lots of companies offer tandem flights and equipment hire, including *Tenerfly (flights from 90 euros | C/ Reykjavik | Adeje | tel. 637 55 92 22 | www.tenerfly.com).*

RIDING

There is a riding stable at the *Amarilla Golf & Country Club (Autopista del Sur, exit at Los Abrigos, Km 3 | tel. 922 73 03 19 | amarillagolf.es)* near Los Abrigos. Several *fincas* specialise in riding holidays. The *Finca Estrella (Fuente de Vega 24 | tel. 922 81 43 82 | www.teneriffa-reiten.com/text/english)* near Icod de los Vinos offers hacks in the unspoilt woodland nearby.

SURFING

There are excellent surfing opportunities on the north coast; however, the best place is *Playa de Benijo*, beyond the Anaga Mountains, although it can take a long time to get there. A good spot for beginners is *Playa de Martiánez* in Puerto de la Cruz. More experienced surfers are well served at *Playa del Socorro* or *Playa Punta Brava*, west of Puerto de la Cruz. Conditions are also ideal off *El Médano* in the south. There is a surf

Surfers get their kicks on the Atlantic swell

Hiking in Parque Nacional del Teide

school in Puerto de la Cruz at Playa Martiánez *(lamareasurfschool.com)*.

WALKING

The most beautiful hiking areas include *Valle de la Orotava*, the *Anaga* and *Teno* mountain ranges and *Parque Nacional del Teide*. And in the south, there is the enticing *Barranco del Infierno*. Most trails are well sign-posted but the terrain is often steep so make sure you're well prepared and in good physical shape before you set off. Inexperienced hikers can join a guided walk. There are plenty to pick from, including *Sergio Walking Tours* *(sergiowalkingtours.com)* who also leads tours from a four-star hotel in the quiet village of *Los Silos (Luz del Mar | Av. Sibora 10 | La Caleta | tel. 922 84 16 23 | luzdelmar. de/en | €€)*, the hotel is perfectly located to explore the countryside. They offer tours at all levels or you can hire maps and GPS phones if you prefer to explore alone.

The big resorts all have agencies offering English-speaking guides and tours at differing levels.

WINDSURFING

The hot spots are mainly along the southeast coast. With wind strengths in winter usually around 5, in summer as high as 8, experienced windsurfers love it here. *El Cabezo* and *La Jaquita* (wind strengths 4–8) are only suitable for experts. World championship events are staged in the inshore waters near *El Médano* (wind strengths 3–5).

The *Surf Center (C/ La Gaviota | tel. 922 17 66 88 | surfcenter.el-medano. com)* offers wind- and kitesurfing courses at all levels. They also hire board and storage if you have your own board. The more sheltered

INSIDER TIP
A hiker's paradise

REGIONAL OVERVIEW

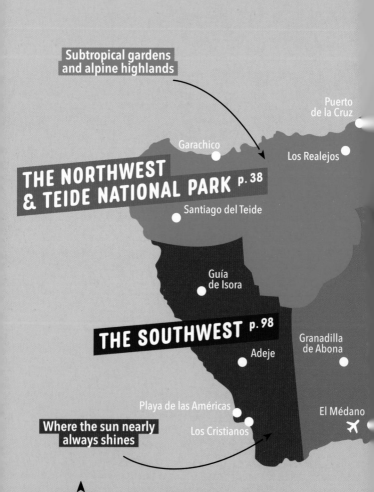

OCÉANO
ATLÁNTICO

Subtropical gardens
and alpine highlands

Puerto
de la Cruz

Garachico

Los Realejos

THE NORTHWEST
& TEIDE NATIONAL PARK p. 38

Santiago del Teide

Guía
de Isora

THE SOUTHWEST p. 98

Granadilla
de Abona

Adeje

Playa de las Américas

El Médano

Where the sun nearly
always shines

Los Cristianos

10 km
6.21 mi

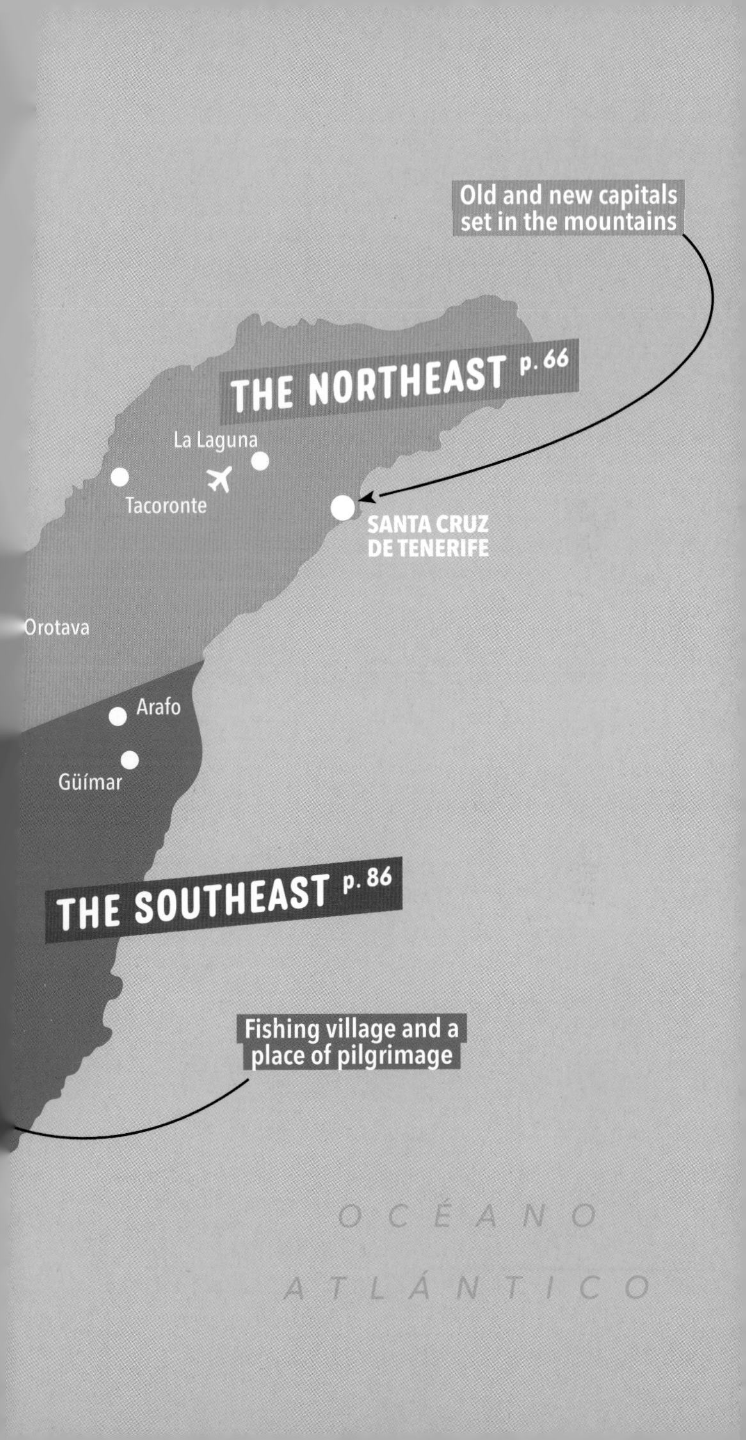

Old and new capitals
set in the mountains

THE NORTHEAST p. 66

La Laguna

Tacoronte

SANTA CRUZ
DE TENERIFE

Orotava

Arafo

Güímar

THE SOUTHEAST p. 86

Fishing village and a
place of pilgrimage

OCÉANO

ATLÁNTICO

THE NORTHWEST & TEIDE NATIONAL PARK

VERDANT VALLEYS & SPAIN'S HIGHEST PEAK

Nowhere else on Tenerife has such a varied landscape as the northwest. Valle de la Orotava is the island's greenest spot thanks to the trade winds, which keep it well supplied with moisture.

When he first set eyes on the valley in 1799, the German explorer, Alexander von Humboldt, wrote "... I have never beheld a prospect more varied, more attractive, more harmonious in the distribution of the masses of verdure and rocks".

Mount Teide rises above the Orotava valley

The valley is no longer so remote. Tourism has brought income but also overdevelopment. Around the northern resort of Puerto de la Cruz ugly hotels blot the coast. However, the further west you go, the more you leave these eyesores behind. In small villages in the shadow of Mount Teide, farmers tend their crops and goats or culti-vate vines as they have for centuries, while the rugged Teno Mountains to the west are a spectacular sight.

THE NORTHWEST & TEIDE NATIONAL PARK

MARCO POLO HIGHLIGHTS

★ **JARDÍN BOTÁNICO**
Exotic plants from all over the world in Puerto de la Cruz's botanical garden ➤ p. 45

★ **LORO PARQUE**
A lot more than just a few parrots (*loros* in Spanish): there are dolphins, seals, penguins and even orcas ➤ p. 46

★ **PLAYA JARDÍN**
Black sand with plenty of palms, waterfalls and little rockpools ➤ p. 48

★ **CASAS DE LOS BALCONES**
La Orotava's grand houses have delightful patios that are well worth admiring ➤ p. 52

★ **CORPUS CHRISTI**
Carpets made from volcanic sand are rolled out in La Orotava every year to celebrate the festival of Corpus Christi ➤ p. 54

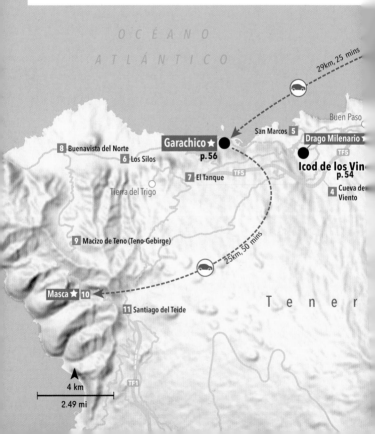

OCÉANO
ATLÁNTICO

29km, 25 mins

Buen Paso

San Marcos **5**

Garachico ★
p. 56

Drago Milenario ➤

TF5

Icod de los Vin
p. 54

8 Buenavista del Norte

6 Los Silos

7 El Tanque   TF5

4 Cueva de
Viento

Tierra del Trigo

9 Macizo de Teno (Teno-Gebirge)

25km, 50 mins

Masca ★ **10**

11 Santiago del Teide

T e n e r

4 km

2.49 mi

TF1

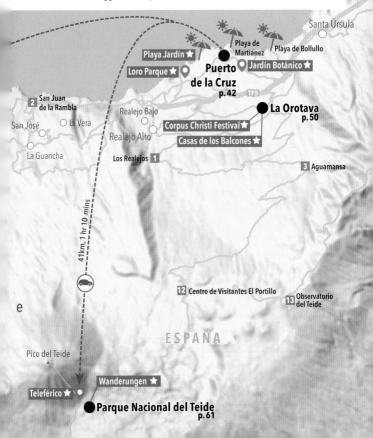

★ **DRAGO MILENARIO**
Icod de los Vinos is home to what is reputedly the oldest dragon tree in the world ➤ p. 54

★ **GARACHICO**
Historic Old Town, wild and windswept coast, a castle and good restaurants ➤ p. 56

★ **MASCA**
A stunning village built of mountain stone lies hidden between rugged cliffs ➤ p. 60

★ **TELEFÉRICO**
A spectacular cable car ride to the top of Spain's highest mountain ➤ p. 63

★ **WALKING**
The unique natural world at Las Cañadas in the national park will take your breath away ➤ p. 65

Santa Úrsula

Playa de Martiánez

Playa de Bollullo

Playa Jardín ★

Loro Parque ★

Puerto de la Cruz p. 42

Jardín Botánico ★

TF5

San Juan de la Rambla 2

La Vera

Realejo Bajo

La Orotava p. 50

San José

Realejo Alto

Corpus Christi Festival ★

La Guancha

Los Realejos 1

Casas de los Balcones ★

3 Aguamansa

41km, 1 hr 10 mins

12 Centro de Visitantes El Portillo

13 Observatorio del Teide

e

ESPAÑA

Pico del Teide

Wanderungen ★

Teleférico ★

Parque Nacional del Teide p. 61

PUERTO DE LA CRUZ

OCÉANO ATLÁNTICO

Calle Mequínez

Casa de la Real Aduana

Puerto Pesquero

Casa Museo d

Calle Santo Domingo

Calle Qu

Calle Mequínez

Museo Arqueológico Municipal

El Templo del Vino

Mundo del Mapa

Ig
de

El Taller Seve Díaz

Casa
Régulo

Plaza del Charco

Calle San Felipe

Calle Puerto Viejo

Calle Mazaroco

Calle Colagan

Calle el Peñón

Calle Doctor Ingram

Calle Iriarte

Luis Lavaggi

Llarena

Calle Cupido

Calle Blanco

Calle

Castillo San Felipe

Paseo

Av. M. del Campo

Calle El Pozo

Avenida Melchor

Hermanos Fernández Perdigón

Calle Cabezas

Playa Jardín ★

Luz

Mercado Municipal

Paseo

Calle Las Cabezas

Avenida Blas Pérez González

Loro Parque ★

Taoro

Carretera

Parque Taoro

PUERTO DE LA CRUZ

(□ G–H 4–5) **Huge ugly buildings are surrounded by lush parks, crowded streets, bright swimming pools, seedy neon signs and grand colonial buildings, and old men pass the time of day on grand plazas. Puerto de la Cruz struggles to** find the right balance between the past and the present and is still working out how best to manage its tourism business.

By 1900, the British had discovered this cool spot and its pleasant climate and claimed it for themselves. The first hotels were built in grand gardens above the fishing village, which until then had been used by the Spanish as a port for exporting sugar cane and wine from the Orotava Valley.

There were elegant hotels like the casino hotel Taoro, which still sits proudly above the town. Many Canary islanders only settled here once tourism had become established; since the 1960s the spa hotels have been joined by huge hotel complexes and guesthouses.

Unlike the resorts in the south, locals and tourists have to rub along here, and the town does its best to meet the needs of its 45,000 inhabitants as well as the demands of the hundreds of thousands of holiday-makers who flock here each year. Between Playa de Martiánez in the east and Plaza del Charco in the centre, you will find many shops and restaurants, modern glass office buildings as well as examples of colonial architecture and squares to relax in.

WHERE TO START?

The nicest bits of Puerto are down at the water's edge and on its "second floor" around the Parque Taoro. As the town sprawls for several kilometres along the coast, it is worth making sure you take the right exit *(salida)* from the TF-5 motorway: Salida 32 for the *Jardín Botánico* and *La Paz* area; Salida 35 for *Parque Taoro*; Salida 35 or 36 for *Playa Jardín*; Salida 39 for *Loro Parque*. Caution: there are not many car parks but there is an underground one at the *Centro Comercial Pirámides de Martiánez* (Salida 32).

SIGHTSEEING

PLAZA DEL CHARCO

Puerto de la Cruz's main square, the rectangular Plaza del Charco, is the place where the locals like to gather for a chat in the shade of Canary palms and Indian laurel trees while children run around in the playground. Notice the *Rincón del Puerto*, a building in Canarian style dating from 1739 with wooden balconies and a luxuriously planted patio, now shared by two restaurants.

IGLESIA DE NUESTRA SEÑORA DE LA PEÑA DE FRANCIA

Built in 1697, Puerto's main church is situated on the elevated *Plaza de la Iglesia*. It has a heavily gilded altarpiece on the Baroque main altar and stunning statues of several saints,

including the *Virgen del Rosario* and the *Virgen de los Dolores*. *C/ Quintana*

CASA DE LA REAL ADUANA

One of the oldest buildings in Puerto de la Cruz is the Royal Customs House. Built in 1620, its wooden windows and balconies perfectly exemplify Canarian architecture. It ceased to function as a customs house 150 years ago. Now the ground floor of the building houses a tourist office and *Artenerife* shop selling local handicrafts, while the upstairs is home to the *Museum of Contemporary Art (MACEW)*, which shows work by Canarian artists, including some particularly expressive local painters like Juan Ismael and surrealist Óscar Domínguez. *Mon–Fri 10am-5.30pm, Sat 10am–1pm | admission free | C/ Las Lonjas 1 | ⏱ 30 mins*

INSIDER TIP
Beautifully odd

CASA MUSEO DEL PESCADOR 🐷

This "fisherman's house" is jam-packed with model ships, stuffed fish and a host of skeletons as well as old photos of life on the high seas. *Daily 9am–7pm | admission free | C/ las Lonjas 5 | ⏱ 30 mins*

PUERTO PESQUERO

The narrow fishing harbour lies opposite the Plaza del Charco. You will be greeted by the *Pescadora*, a life-size bronze statue of a woman carrying a basket on her head. When the boats arrive back in port, buyers emerge amid a bustle of activity and the noisy haggling over the day's catch begins.

Art and culture are protected behind the thick walls of Castillo San Felipe

MUSEO ARQUEOLÓGICO MUNICIPAL

On the west side of the Plaza del Charco stands the town's Archaeological Museum with a collection of Guanche mummies, weapons and historical maps. *Tue–Sat 10am–1pm and 5–9pm, Sun 10am–1pm | admission 2 euros (Thu free) | C/ del Lomo 9a | ⊙ 30 mins*

CASTILLO SAN FELIPE

San Felipe castle is just under 1 km from the centre of town. It was built between 1630 and 1644 to defend the island from pirates, hence the intimidating cannon by the entrance. The building is now used for cultural events and exhibitions. There's a huge rockery and a view over Playa Jardín. *Tue–Sat 11am–1pm and 5–8pm | admission free | Paseo de Luis Lavaggi | ⊙ 30 mins*

PARQUE TAORO 🐗

The first grand hotels were built for mainly British spa guests at the end of the 19th century on this plateau overlooking the sea and the town. The park covers 10 hectares and consists of gardens, footpaths, lookouts, waterfalls, fountains, a playground and a restaurant. Within the grounds behind the former Taoro Casino Hotel is a beautiful, terraced garden. Known as the *Risco Bello*, it boasts a fine array of flowers, fruits, an ivy-covered grotto and a *Jardín Acuático* with plenty of ponds. *Admission to the park is free, Risco Bello 4 euros | Altos de Taoro*

JARDÍN BOTÁNICO ★

Tropical plants of every kind. Cinnamon trees, sausage trees, strangler figs, pepper and tulip trees, coral and breadfruit trees, coffee and cocoa bushes, araucaria, various fruit trees and a fig tree as tall as a church – you can see all of this and much more at the Botanical Garden. It was built by King Carlos III in 1790 on 2.5 hectares of land to help exotic plants from the tropics adjust to the temperate climate of Europe. The second stage of this ambitious plan, i.e. to introduce these plants to the Spanish mainland, was less successful as plants that flourished in tropical climates did not like the cool winters of Madrid. *Daily 9am–6pm | admission 4.50 euros | C/ Retama 2 | ⏱ 1 hr*

LAGO MARTIÁNEZ 😙

César Manrique, the brilliant landscape architect from Lanzarote, designed a swimming area here

Enjoy a glass of wine in the Templo del Vino

between the cliffs with waterfalls fountains and big seawater swimming pools all set in green surroundings. *Daily 10am–5pm | admission 5.50 euros, children (up to 10) 2.50 euros | Costa Martiánez | ociocostamartianez. com*

LORO PARQUE ★ 😙

The biggest zoo on the Canary Islands. With everything from gorillas to lions and Bengal tigers, there is plenty to see here. In the huge bird enclosures, there are rope bridges and ladders allowing you to get up close to the animals. A vast, snow-filled dome houses two different species of penguin and there is an aquarium in a tunnel meaning you can get very close to over 20,000 species of fish, sharks and rays. And there are dolphin, sea lion and orca shows every day. The park offers Discovery Tours which allow you to get behind the scenes **INSIDER TIP** *For the full experience ..* and learn far more about the animals. *Daily 8.30am–6.45pm (last entry) | admission 34 euros, children (4–11) 23 euros, discount on second visit; combined ticket with Siam Park 58 euros, children 39.50 euros | Playa Punta Brava (free mini-train every 20 mins from Playa de Martiánez) | loro parque.com | ⏱ 4 hrs*

EATING & DRINKING

BAMBI GOURMET

Hidden away in a side street yet always well frequented, Bambi Gourmet serves a variety of freshly made Spanish dishes and Romanian specialities in a cosy atmosphere. *Closed Sun | C/ Enrique Talg 15 | tel. 922 38 38 87 | bambi-gourmet.es | €€*

CAFÉ ALBA

Tuck into snacks, salads and sweets with a stunning view of the coast. Their home-made lemonade is delicious and you can put your detective skills to the test too: there is a statue of Agatha Christie nearby. Can you find her? *(Mirador La Paz). C/ Pitera 5 | tel. 922 37 10 54 | €*

CASA RÉGULO

Imaginative, multiple award-winning Canarian cuisine in a renovated mansion. Try the octopus carpaccio *(carpaccio de pulpo). Closed Sun | C/ Pérez Zamora 16 | tel. 922 38 45 06 | €€€*

EL TALLER SEVE DÍAZ

"Seve's workshop" is a small, elegant restaurant in Puerto's dining district. You'll be greeted with an *amuse bouche* from the kitchen and home-made bread, followed by creative Canarian dishes that will delight both your eyes and your palate. Ideal for a special evening! *Wed–Sun 7-10.30pm, Sat, Sun also 1–3pm | C/ San Felipe 32 | tel. 822 25 75 38 | €€-€€€*

EL TEMPLO DEL VINO

A near religious drinking (and eating) experience: exquisite Canarian wines served with delicious tapas. If you are very hungry, order a kebab which comes served (ominously) "on the gallows"! *Closed Tue | C/ del Lomo 2 | tel. 922 37 41 64 | templodelvino.com | €€*

SHOPPING

CALLE QUINTANA

You'll find everything – from art galleries to supermarkets – in the pedestrianised heart of the Old Town. The *Columbus Plaza* shopping centre has an attractive patio and shops selling everything from the latest fashions to cigars and perfumes.

MERCADO MUNICIPAL

The concrete market hall is not a pretty sight. But it still attracts many shoppers looking for fresh local produce. If you're craving whole-grain bread and good cake, visit *Harry's Gourmetería* upstairs. There is also a flea market here on Wednesdays and Saturdays 10am–2pm. *Mon–Sat 8am–2pm and 4–8pm | C/ Blas Pérez González 6 | mercadopuertodelacruz.es*

THE ENGLISH LIBRARY

Inviting shop (despite limited opening hours) with an excellent selection of English books, puzzles and souvenirs. Its small café and charming garden are also a great place to meet local expats and tourists alike. *Wed/Sat 10am-1pm | C/ Irlanda 5*

SPORT & ACTIVITIES

CYCLING

If you want to get around Puerto de la Cruz by bicycle, you can hire mountain bikes opposite the bus station from 65 euros for three days at *MTB Active (C/ Puerto Viejo 44/Dr Madan (next to the Hotel San Borondón) | mobile tel. 669 15 75 67 (9–11am) and 620 00 59 98 (4.30–6.30pm) | mtb-active.com).*

LEARN SOME SPANISH

The boutique hotel *Puerto Azul* is attached to *Sothis Language School (C/ del Lomo 24 | tel. 922 38 32 13 | short.travel/ten4)* where you can take courses at all levels and intensities.

INSIDER TIP
Hablas español?

WELLNESS

ORIENTAL SPA GARDEN

Puerto's nicest Spa is the *Hotel Botánico*'s Oriental Garden. It welcomes non-residents and has thalasso pools alongside jacuzzis outside, and a range of saunas, steam rooms, flotation tanks and therapeutic showers in a series of caves inside. All set in a pretty garden with a fishpond and pagoda. *Daily 9am–8pm | C/ Richard J Yeoward 1 | treatments from 42 euros | tel. 922 38 95 05 | orientalspagarden.com*

BEACHES

PLAYA DE BOLLULLO

This 200-m-long, pitch-black beach is hidden away beneath steep picturesque cliffs 4km to the east of Puerto de la Cruz. There is also a beach bar for refreshments.

PLAYA DE MARTIÁNEZ

The almost untouched town beach (250m long) to the east of Puerto de la Cruz is composed of coarse, black sand with outcrops of volcanic rock. There's a boardwalk for walkers and the view along the north coast is incredible.

PLAYA JARDÍN ★

It is called "Garden Beach" for a reason. With a waterpark, lush tropical flora, and lots of caves, this is a charming spot. It looks so pretty and natural that it's hard to believe it is artificial – they had to bring in 200,000m³ of dark volcanic sand as well as building an underwater reef to stop the sand being washed away. There are lots of cafés and restaurants catering to your every need.

NIGHTLIFE

Plaza del Charco is a popular spot, with bars, cafés and ice cream parlours. *Dinámico (open daily)* on the square is an open-sided pavilion with a large bar, lots of tables and a good selection of drinks and snacks. Around the corner the rustic *Bodega Julián (C/ Mequinez 20 | tel. 686 55 63 15 | €€)* serves good food to the sound of live Latin American and Spanish music.

Night owls will inevitably find themselves heading towards Lago de Martiánez. *Café de París (Av. de Colón 2)* has a terrace and serves cocktails until midnight. Things only get lively after midnight and at weekends in the area around *Calle La Hoya* and the intersecting *Av. Familia Betancourt y Molina*.

Abaco (C/ Casa Grande | Urbanización El Durazno | tel. 922 37

01 07 | *abacotenerife.com*) offers a more unusual form of entertainment above Puerto de la Cruz. It's a superbly restored country estate, which you can also visit during the day *(Tue–Sun 10am–1.30pm folklore shows | admission 9 euros)*. In the evening they serve exotic (expensive) cocktails at the bar, in cosy seating areas, or on wicker chairs in the romantic gardens. And there are also regular classical concerts.

If you feel the need to boost your holiday funds, you can always try your luck at the *casino (Mon–Wed and Fri 8pm–4am, Sun and Thu 8pm–3am | admission free (bring some ID) | tel. 922 38 05 50 | casinostenerife.com)*.

AROUND PUERTO DE LA CRUZ

■ LOS REALEJOS

10km/10 mins southwest of Puerto de la Cruz on the TF-333

West of Puerto de la Cruz, the municipality of Los Realejos (pop. 36,000) is an amalgamation of several small villages spread over steep ridges and separated by deep canyons. Tenerife's first church (1496) *Santiago Apóstol*, is testimony to this area's former wealth – today's testaments are large hotels.

Playa Jardín: the black-sand "garden beach" of Puerto de la Cruz at the foot of Mount Teide

The restaurant *El Monasterio (daily | La Vera | C/ La Montaña | tel. 922 34 07 07 | mesonelmonasterio.com | €–€€)* occupies the premises of a former monastery in La Montañeta, close to Puerto de la Cruz. Small animals roam freely in the grounds, which are beautifully landscaped with plenty of greenery. Guests can choose between typical Canarian cuisine in the superb restaurant or light snacks in the cafeteria.

Beneath the village of La Guancha you can visit the *Bodega Viñátigo (Mon–Fri 10am–1pm, 2.30–5.30pm | registration necessary | 1.5km from La Guancha on TF-352 | C/ Travesía Juandana | vinatigo.com).* This modern winery has used beautiful natural stone to create a stunning tasting room. *G5*

INSIDER TIP
A stylish place to sip

☑ SAN JUAN DE LA RAMBLA
14km/17 mins west of Puerto de la Cruz on the TF-5

It won't take long to walk through all the alleys of this historic, somewhat sleepy town. More excitement can be found in the fishermen's quarter *Las Aguas*, where waves incessantly pound against the cliffs. It's not only nice to look at; it'll awaken your appetite, which you can satisfy at a Las Aguas restaurant *(closed Mon | C/ La Destila 20 | tel. 922 36 04 28 | €)*, located in a country house above the promenade. *F5*

LA OROTAVA

(☐ H5) **Grand town houses line steep narrow lanes while elegant mansions with spacious, dark-wood balconies surround large squares.**

Ignore the traffic and new housing developments on the outskirts, and you'll think you're back in colonial times! It is no surprise that at the beginning of the 16th century the Spaniards decided to build a town here. With water bubbling from the many springs, this was the lushest part of the green *Valle de la Orotava* and its fertile soil provided bountiful harvests. They planted sugar cane which was then shipped from the port, Puerto de la Orotava (now Puerto de la Cruz), all over the world, and as a result amassed considerable wealth.

Although earthquakes in 1704 and 1705 destroyed large parts of the town it was immediately rebuilt. That explains why the historic centre remains largely intact and has been spared any modern architectural monstrosities. Today, it is protected as a part of Europe's cultural heritage. Tourism in *La Orotava* (pop. 40,000) is mainly restricted to day visitors strolling through the Old Town with its fine squares. But there's plenty of attractive accommodation, so you could stay a bit longer …

SIGHTSEEING

PLAZA DE LA CONSTITUCIÓN
The pavilion in the middle of Constitution Square is the heart of La

Orotava. The square is generously pro-portioned and always beautifully planted with flowers and shrubs. It is surrounded by a number of historical buildings – such as *San Agustín*, a for-mer convent dating back to 1671, and the *Liceo de Taoro*, a palace painted rust red which is now a private cultural centre. There's a great view from the plaza too, with the town spreading out at your feet!

PLAZA DEL AYUNTAMIENTO

La Orotava's main square, overlooked by seven towering Canary palm trees, extends out from town hall. This is the stage for all the major festivals, includ-ing the colourful Corpus Christi celebrations. Around Christmas, a beautiful life-size Nativity scene adorns one of the neighbouring streets *(C/ Isla de la Gomera 7)*.

HIJUELA DEL BOTÁNICO

The "little daughter" *(hijuela)* of the Puerto de la Cruz botanical garden is hidden behind the town hall, and at 4,000m² really is quite small. But it's still worth a visit to see the Australian conifers, Indian chestnut trees, flame trees (flamboyants) and a lovely dragon tree. Some plants date back to the foundation of the garden in 1788. *Mon–Sat 9am–6pm | admission free | C/ Tomás Pérez*

JARDINES DEL MARQUESADO DE LA QUINTA ROJA

Above Hijuela del Botánico, a pretty park climbs up the terraced slope.

The pretty pavilion on Plaza de la Constitución is the place to be in La Orotava

Passing by exotic plants, each more magnificent and colourful than the one before, you will reach the Marqués de la Quinta Roja's marble mausoleum and will be able to enjoy a panorama of the town from above. *Daily 9am–6pm | admission free*

PARROQUIA DE LA INMACULADA CONCEPCIÓN DE LA VIRGEN MARÍA

Less is more? Not here, where it's all about pomp! Two bell towers flank a massive, richly decorated Baroque façade. And that's just a taste of the splendour that awaits you inside. The three naves are divided by pillars and a mighty dome arches up over the crossing. It lets in just enough light to make the jasper and marble altar below shimmer mysteriously. The Church of the Immaculate Conception was consecrated to the Virgin Mary in 1788. It was meant to surpass the beauty of its predecessor destroyed in the 1704–05 earthquakes: "What the destructive forces of nature take from us, we will rebuild all the more splendidly!" *Plaza Casañas*

CASAS DE LOS BALCONES ★

Plain but elegant houses face each other in *Calle San Francisco*. They get their name, *Casas de los Balcones*, from their wonderful and finely crafted wooden balconies – a typical characteristic of Canarian buildings. The balconies look as though they have been glued on to the façade. The first, *Casa Fonseca* (1632) enchants

visitors with its bright green patio and an arcade panelled entirely with wood on the first floor. The rooms are now used by an embroidery school whose fabrics and bedspreads are on sale (after you have watched them being made). In 1670 the equally fine house next door, *Casa de Franchi*, was built; it now houses a carpet museum *(Museo de las Alfombras)*. However, these are not woven rugs but floor coverings made from volcanic sand, as seen in the Corpus Christi celebrations.

Opposite is *Casa Molina*, formerly a monastery dating from 1590. It now houses one of the island's largest craft shops. *casa-balcones.com*.

RUTA DE LOS MOLINOS DE AGUA

No fewer than nine waterwheels were built to take advantage of La Orotava's abundance of water. Built in the 16th century, they were still being used

Casas de los Balcones: wooden balconies in the green courtyard of Casa Fonseca

well into the 20th century. Built in a row along streets that climbed steeply up the hillside, their job was to grind *gofio*, the Canarian staple (see p. 26). They were linked by channels that carried water from the Araujo stream and then from one mill to the next. Seven of the mills and parts of the channels can still be seen.

One of the three mills that are still working – *C/ Domingo González García 3* – is now powered by electricity and continues to grind (and sell) fresh *gofio* every day. *Mon–Fri 8am–1pm and 3–7pm, Sat 8am–1pm | Start of route: south of the Casas de los Balcones*

INSIDER TIP
It tastes best fresh

CENTRO DE VISITANTES TELESFORO BRAVO DEL PARQUE
The National Park Information Centre is not just the place to get permits to climb Mount Teide. They also have an exhibition about local flora and upstairs you can admire the gigantic volcano. *Tue–Sun 9am–2pm and 3.30–6pm | admission free | C/ Sixto Perera 25 | El Mayorazgo | junction 34 | tel. 922 92 23 71 | reservasparques nacionales.es*

MUSEO DE ARTESANÍA IBEROAMERICANA
There is an arts and crafts museum in the former Dominican monastery of Santo Domingo, which dates from the 17th century. You will see traditional costumes, instruments and beautiful objects from Spain and the New World. The monastery's cloister is a masterpiece of simplicity. *Mon–Fri 10am–3pm | admission 3 euros | C/ Tomás Zerolo 34*

EATING & DRINKING

SABOR CANARIO
"Canarian flavour" *(sabor canario)* in a historic stately home in the Old Town. The chefs here are passionate about traditional fare — from *rancho* to *bienmesabe*. *Closed Sun | C/ Carrera 17 | tel. 922 32 27 25 | €–€€*

SHOPPING

CASA DE LOS BALCONES AND CASA DEL TURISTA
These two shops sell a wide range of souvenirs and tasty delicacies. However, not everything is locally sourced. *Mon–Sat 9am–6.30pm (Casa de los Balcones also Sun) | C/ San Fernando 3 and 4*

CASA TORREHERMOSA
Certified (collector's) items made by Tenerife's artisans. *Artenerife (Mon–Fri 10am–3pm | C/ Tomás Zerolo 27)* is housed in a 17th-century mansion.

FESTIVALS

CORPUS CHRISTI ★
Carpets made from lava? At Corpus Christi (see Festivals & events, p. 139) you will see these on show in La Orotava's biggest festival. These huge "carpets" portray biblical scenes using lots of different coloured volcanic sand. The finest of them all is displayed at the town hall on Plaza de la Constitución.

AROUND LA OROTAVA

🗷 AGUAMANSA
13km/15 mins southeast of La Orotava on TF-21
Beyond the village of Aguamansa, about halfway between La Orotava and the Parque Nacional del Teide, there is a dense pine forest where you can park up and look back up the Orotava Valley. On the left-hand side you will find a picnic spot in a crater, *La Caldera*. From there, signposted walking trails head off in all directions. ⏛ *J5*

ICOD DE LOS VINOS

(⏛ E5) **Is it crazy to visit a place because of one tree? If that's your reason for coming to Icod de los Vinos, you won't be alone. Thousands arrive every year to see the best dragon trees on the island.**

Although ★ ⚑ the *Drago Milenario* does not date back 1,000 years as the name suggests, its age is estimated at 500 to 600 years, making it the oldest dragon tree in the world. With a diameter of 6m and a height of 17m , it is also unsurpassed in size. It occupies a prominent position in the middle of town in its own botanic garden, the *Parque del Drago* (daily 9am–6pm | admission 5 euros | *Plaza de la Constitución 1*). The garden has a "Guanche trail", where you learn about the island's original inhabitants.

Going for a stroll through Icod (pop. 23,000) can be fun too. Founded in 1501, vines were quickly planted on its fertile hills. Many bodegas offering tastings still line the streets and plazas of the Old Town.

SIGHTSEEING

IGLESIA SAN MARCOS

The 15th-century *San Marcos* church sits on Icod's pretty main square, the *Plaza Lorenzo Cáceres*, near the Parque del Drago. Through its Renaissance portal you'll enter the dimly lit interior with its carved wooden ceiling. Make sure you take in the silver-embossed Baroque altar. Even more silver lies in the Treasury. The *Plaza de Pila* with its 18th-century houses is just a few metres away and is home to some nice wine shops.

MUSEO MUÑECAS/ARTLANDYA

The place is as eccentric and beautiful as the exhibition itself. Hundreds of dolls designed by acclaimed designers are exhibited in a colourful hacienda. You can find out how the dolls are made on an English-language tour of the workshop.

INSIDER TIP
Return to childhood

The *Drago Milenario* in Icod de los Vinos

Oh, and there are teddy bears in all shapes and sizes to see too … *Tue–Sun 10am–6pm | admission 10 euros | Camino el Moleiro 21 | 3km to the east of Santa Bárbara | artlandya.com*

EATING & DRINKING

CARMEN

It can get fairly cool in Icod. The perfect way to get warm is with a hearty spicy cress soup – *potaje de berros*! And the rustic atmosphere with lots of wood will warm up your heart too. *Daily | C/ Hércules 2 | tel. 922 81 06 31 | €€*

AROUND ICOD DE LOS VINOS

4 CUEVA DEL VIENTO ☂

5km/10 mins south of Icod on the TF-366

If you want to climb into the bowels of a volcano, you've come to the right place. At a small visitor centre, you will receive an introduction into how the "cave of the wind" came into being. It was formed 27,000 years ago, when the Pico Viejo erupted and sent trails of lava flowing down into the valley. The lava cooled rapidly on the surface, while underneath it kept flowing, thereby creating tunnels. At 17km in length, this is one of the longest lava tubes in the world. In eternal darkness, only highly adaptable creatures have been able to make a home here, including a blind cockroach – don't worry, it's totally harmless! *Tue–Sat 9am–4pm | admission 20 euros | visits (2hrs) three times per day in Spanish and English for small groups | C/ los Piquetes 51 | pre-booking essential: tel. 922 81 53 39 | cuevadelviento. net | sturdy shoes required ⬜ E6*

5 SAN MARCOS

2 km/5 mins north of Icod on the TF-414

INSIDER TIP
A pretty beach all to yourselves

One of the few beaches to swim at in the north. About 100m long, the beach of pitch-black volcanic sand is deserted on weekdays, but on Saturday and Sunday it fills up with hundreds of islanders who come here to swim, spend the weekend in the nearby apartments and keep the small, local restaurants busy. One of them, a *Casa María (daily | tel. 922 81 05 33 | €–€€)* is on the promenade overlooking sea and beach. Their speciality — like almost everywhere else here — is fish. *⬜ E5*

GARACHICO

(⬜ D5) **Beautiful architecture, terrific natural surroundings – ★ life is good in Garachico! Cobblestone alleys lined with historic buildings lead to a plaza with monasteries, churches and old laurels trees.**

Immediately behind, cliffs rise to heights of 1,000m, and on the volcanic coast, naturally formed pools offer a place to take a dip – don't get in unless it's calm! Garachico (pop. 5,700) is idyllic – despite a major disaster in 1706 when mighty streams of lava erupted from the "Black Volcano" and flowed down across a broad front over the cliffs and into the sea, burying one of Tenerife's main ports. But something new emerged: the hot lava cooled in the waters of the Atlantic, where it conveniently formed *Isla Baja*, or "low island" and the locals defiantly rebuilt their new town on the only recently cooled lava.

A stroll through the Old Town, which still has some lovely buildings that miraculously survived the

Don't miss the Plaza de Pila on your walk around Icod de los Vinos

eruptions, is like being in an open-air museum.

SIGHTSEEING

CASTILLO DE SAN MIGUEL

Inconceivable, but true: this tiny castle once protected Garachico from pirate attacks. The portal, adorned with coats of arms, was built in 1575. Enter through it and imagine being on the "upper deck" of the fortification and waiting for an enemy armada ... *Daily 10am–6pm | admission 1.50 euros | Av. Tomé Cano*

CONVENTO DE SAN FRANCISCO

Here too you'll find yourself transported back in time, to the year 1524. In this Franciscan monastery, you can walk as the monks once did through romantic cloisters and enter rooms with delicate stone flooring and stunning Mudéjar ceilings. Alongside the relics, you'll find a relief model of Tenerife marking the locations of lava flows in recent centuries. There are also multimedia installations showing all the Earth's hotspots of volcanic activity. Next door, the *Casa de la Cultura* has temporary art exhibitions. *Mon–Fri 10am–7pm, Sat, Sun 10am–3pm | admission 1 euro | Plaza de la Libertad*

IGLESIA DE SANTA ANA

The main church (1520) is just three steps away from the convent. Here too, you'll find wooden Mudéjar ceilings and lava-stone pillars in the dimly lit

El Caletón, Garachico's natural swimming pool

space. The sorrowful and suffering saints at the main altar were carved by Luján Pérez, the Canaries' star sculptor in the 18th century. And take a look at the clock, which has been ticking with Swiss precision since time immemorial! *Mon–Sat 10am–5pm | admission 2 euros*

EL CALETÓN NATURAL SWIMMING POOLS

Need a cool down after your walk? The streams of lava that cooled down in the sea are not only picturesque; they have also created natural bathing pools. When the sea is calm (but only then!), you can use the steps and metal ladders to climb down from the rocks into the sea for a swim.

EATING & DRINKING

ARDEOLA

Take a seat on the promenade to enjoy creative Canarian cuisine in simple yet elegant surroundings. *INSIDER TIP* **Avant garde and traditional** Ask Señor Ángel for the fish of the day! The restaurant's *milhoja de papas*, vegetable tartar sprinkled with goat's cheese, is particularly delicious. *Daily 6–10pm, Sat/Sun also 1–4pm | Av. Tomé Cano 4 | tel. 922 13 3012 | restauranteardeola.com | €€*

CASA GASPAR

One of the best spots around – and has been for many years – serving meat from the grill and fresh fish (priced according to weight), fast and friendly service. *Closed Sun, Mon | C/ Esteban del Ponte 44 | tel. 922 83 00 40 | €€*

SHOPPING

ARTSHOP
Everything here is made by local artists who have found inspiration on the island. Guanche-style pottery, lava-stone jewellery, paintings and photos. *C/ Esteban Ponte 3 | artshop-garachico. com*

AROUND GARACHICO

6 LOS SILOS
6km/5 mins west of Garachico on the TF-42
A tiered white church on a plaza with a pavilion forms the centre of the pleasantly sleepy village of Los Silos (pop. 5,500). Diagonally opposite the church in an old convent is an attractive visitor centre. The *Centro de Visitantes (Mon–Fri 9am–1pm, Sat 9am–2pm | admission free | Plaza de la Luz 10)* provides helpful information on local geology, flora and fauna, and walking opportunities in the Teno Mountains.

The road ends at a much-too-tall apartment block – an eyesore in otherwise stunning surroundings. As there are no local beaches, there's a swimming pool here where you can swim a few lengths, while looking longingly at the ocean. There is also a 15-m-long skeleton of a pollack whale that got stranded here in 2005 – now it's a symbol for the conservation of sea life. *C5*

7 EL TANQUE
6km/12 mins southwest of Garachico on the TF-421/TF-82
The next village up from Garachico may not look like much, but it has a very unusual attraction. The 🐫 *Camello Center* offers guided tours through the volcanic landscape … on camels. To make the whole thing more surreal, they dress you up in Bedouin clothing . The ride lasts just 20 minutes but afterwards you can visit the goats, ponies and donkeys in the petting zoo. There is also a restaurant offering traditional food. Be aware that if you arrive at the same time as a big tour bus, waiting times can be extremely long. *Daily 10am–5pm | admission 10 euros, children (aged 3–12) 5 euros | El Tanque | TF-82, Km10.2 | tel. 922 13 61 91 | camello center.es | D5*

8 BUENAVISTA DEL NORTE
11km/10 mins west of Garachico on the TF-42
The name says it all: *buena vista* ("good view") over rugged cliffs and the vast Atlantic. Tenerife's most westerly town (pop. 5,400) is tucked in beneath the impressive *Teno Mountains*. The TF-445 heads west to *Buenavista Golf (green fee: 1 round 75 euros | tel. 922 12 90 34 | buena vistagolf.es)*, an 18-hole golf course in

The pretty village of Masca sits hidden among the Teno mountains

a stunning coastal location. The road carries on past the *Mirador de Don Pompeyo*, which has a spectacular view before it ends at the *Punta de Teno (risk of landslide if wet and windy, Thu–Sun compulsory shuttle service on bus 369 from the church square in Buenavista)*. An old lighthouse stands alongside the new one. On clear days the view extends as far as La Palma and La Gomera. ⏷ *C5*

9 MACIZO DE TENO

20km/30 mins southwest of Garachico

It's hard to believe that the Teno Mountains were once an island on their own. Seven million years ago, they rose from the sea bed and didn't become part of the "main island" around Teide until many more volcanic eruptions connected the two. Even today, the 1,000-m-high Teno Mountains seem remote and

inaccessible with their rugged gorges, steep cliffs and only the occasional green plateau. The *Mirador de Cherfe* on the road from Santiago del Teide to Masca offers a great view of the world from the top of the rugged rocks.

If you love this wild, unspoilt terrain, keep going and then, just south of El Palmar, turn to the west towards *Teno Alto* (⏷ *B6*). You pass a picnic spot and then after 3km, you will reach this remote hamlet spread across a windswept upland plateau. Grazing on the pastures are goats and sheep, whose milk is used to make award-winning cheese. Try this delicacy with a glass of wine in one of the bars on the church square. ⏷ *B–C6*

10 MASCA ★

25km/50 mins southwest of Garachico on the TF-42/TF-436

Even as you approach along the narrow, bendy road, you will barely catch a glimpse of this beautiful village in the middle of the Teno Mountains. The houses, spread across the hillside, were built with blocks of stone hewn from the grey-brown rock found in the surrounding area. The architectural style is typical of the Teno region and Masca is the best example. Until well into the 20th century, ancient shepherd tracks created by the Guanches were the only link with the outside world. They wound along the mountain slopes from village to village as far as Santiago del Teide. A more relaxing way to get to know Masca is to visit either early in the morning or later in the evening, when the place is not overrun by tourists. Below the main road you will find a number of tourist cafés, with terraces overlooking the mountains and the valleys, e.g. *Casa Fidel (closed Thu | tel. 922 86 34 57 | €).* ⏕ *C6-7*

11 SANTIAGO DEL TEIDE

19km/30 mins southwest of Garachico on the TF-82

On the way to the Teno Mountains you'll pass through Santiago. Thios is where the booming holiday resorts around Los Gigantes are managed from – a gold mine for the village. It has a population of 5,400 and is situated on a high plateau with a domed parish church. Right behind it is *La Casona del Patio (Av. de la Iglesia 72 | tel. 922 83 92 93 | lacasonadelpatio. com | €€)*, a venerable winemaking estate that dates back to the year 1663. Two huge traditional wine

INSIDER TIP
Winemaking the old-fashioned way

presses at the entry make it pretty clear what they do here.

Are you interested in traditional handicrafts? Then the hamlet of *Arguayo* south of Santiago is just for you. It was once an important centre for Tenerife's pottery trade. Today the craft only survives at the *Museo del Alfarero (Tue–Sat 10am-1pm, 4-7pm, Sun 10am-2pm | admission free).* This pottery museum is housed in a renovated workshop. Following traditional Guanche methods – i.e. no potter's wheel or tools – all its ceramics are fired in an old kiln. The finished products – simple dishes and pots made from natural clay – are all on sale. The exhibits include some of the finest pieces the potters have produced and some old photographs from the days when business was booming. ⏕ *C7*

PARQUE NACIONAL DEL TEIDE

(⏕ E-H6-8) **Majestic and remote, a trip to Tenerife's national park should be a part of every itinerary. The *Parque Nacional del Teide* reaches impressive altitudes above 2,000m and covers an area of over 135km², making it the largest national park in the Canary Islands. At its heart lies a giant crater by the name of *Las Cañadas*, in the shadow of the almost 4,000-m-high Mount Teide.**

The elliptical Cañadas crater, with a diameter of 16km, is one of the world's largest, with a jagged rocky rim measuring 45km. It's so big it beggars belief. This is a landscape of superlatives. Multicoloured shimmering volcanic rock, broad plains and deep gorges alongside scree slopes – sometimes smooth and polished, sometimes pock-marked. "Mustard Mountain" *(Montaña Mostaza)* shines sulphur yellow and "White Mountain" *(Montaña Blanca)* gleams bright white, while the rounded slag heaps are jet black. Rocks, slammed into the earth, have jagged edges like black glass. Everywhere you go, you'll be surrounded by boulders that look as if they've been strewn by giants. And above it all, the striking peaks. The 3,000-m-high volcanic chimney of the *Pico Viejo* towers on the northern edge of the two craters, where the last major eruption occurred in 1798.

Recent studies suggest, however, that both the Cañadas and the Orotava Valley were formed by landslides of an almost unimaginable scale. Some 1,000m³ of earth fell into the sea during the formation of the Cañadas. It has been established that Mount Teide was formed almost 200,000 years ago, after the landslides, and so in geological terms is still very young.

Don't miss the Roques de García on your walk through the national park

To compare, it was seven million years ago that volcanic activity here raised land from the floor of the Atlantic for the first time, forming one of several islands that would later fuse to make Tenerife.

The apparent lack of vegetation in the national park may make you feel as if you're on another planet. However, this impression is deceptive as 139 species have adjusted to the extreme climatic conditions at high altitude. They have to contend with strong sunshine during the day, freezing temperatures at night and drought. A good 20 per cent of plants are endemic to Tenerife, i.e. they don't

exist anywhere else in the world. These include the pillared *tajinaste rojo* with its bright red flowers (Mount Teide bugloss), the little yellow or white Teide daisy and the Teide violet. Plants at this altitude stay in flower for only a short period, just May and June. Few vertebrates survive in these harsh conditions, with rewilded mouflon sheep, finches and kestrels being among the exceptions.

There are two places you should definitely not miss in the Parque Nacional. First are the *Roques de García* (🗺 F8), an ensemble of multi-coloured rocky outcrops. A viewing platform offers a spectacular view. If you climb a little higher, you will be rewarded with a stunning vista down into the *Llano de Ucanca*, the largest plain in the Teide-Cañadas and also of *Los Azulejos*, a shimmering greenish-blue rock formation.

The second stop is the *Pico del Teide* (🗺 F7) itself, whose almost symmetrical summit reaches a height of 3,718m. Its name is derived from the Guanche word for "hell". Hot sulphur steams out from its slopes, proof that hell still stirs.

The ★ *Teleférico (daily 9am–4pm in good weather, usually closed for maintenance in May | round trip 26 euros | volcanoteide.com | book in advance to avoid queues)*, the Mount Teide cable car, climbs 1,200m to the *La Rambleta* mountain station at 3,550m in 10 minutes. From there you can walk to *La Fortaleza* lookout point and the *Pico Viejo* (3,135m). But be warned: there are often high winds!

Teide Observatory and Institute of Astrophysics

SIGHTS IN THE NATIONAL PARK

12 CENTRO DE VISITANTES EL PORTILLO 🐷

How was the Teide formed? What forces were at work? And how does any life survive in this volcanic desert? The national park's visitor centre – located in a reconstructed lava tube – helps you get to grips with the park. It has an attractive garden around the building where they grow mountain plants that you may encounter in the park itself. *Daily 9am–4pm | admission free| | TF-21| Km32.1 on the northeastern exit of the Cañadas | tel. 922 35 60 00 | ⍌ G6*

13 OBSERVATORIO DEL TEIDE 🚩

A setting worthy of science fiction. These metallic white observatory towers at the eastern entrance stare up into the blue sky, which is so clear that you get a good view of the whole universe. When the Canarian Institute of Astrophysics started its work up here in 1964, it seemed that this spot – well away from civilisation and at an altitude of 2,390m – was the ideal place to view the heavens.

But today the lights from the holiday resorts interfere with the work of the astronomers, so they now observe the night sky from the neighbouring island of La Palma and scientists at Tenerife's Observatory study the sun during the day. On their tours, you can find out how the observatory works and get to look up at the universe through a telescope. *Register at volcanoteide.com | from 21 euros | ⍌ H7–8*

INSIDER TIP
Starlight Express

EATING & DRINKING

PARADOR NACIONAL

The chalet-style *parador* (hotel belonging to a state-run chain) is the highest hotel in the Canaries. Excellent Canarian cuisine in the restaurant or a snack in the café which has a view of El Teide. *Las Cañadas del Teide | tel. 922 38 64 15 | parador.es | €–€€€ | ▥ F8*

SPORT & ACTIVITIES

WALKING ★

Marked walking paths lead through *Las Cañadas* and up to Mount Teide. When climbing Spain's highest mountain, you'll pass by the "Teide Eggs", *Huevos del Teide*, huge boulders of lava rock scattered about the area.

Please be aware, however, that high altitude puts the body under severe strain. Before undertaking longer walks, make sure you are fully acclimatised. Sun protection and plenty of water are essential for all hikes in the national park. You can pick up free information leaflets from the *El Portillo* visitor centre.

WHERE TO STAY

PARK HIDEAWAY

"There is a palm tree for every guest" according to the motto at Tigaiga *(83 rooms and suites | Parque Taoro 28 | tel. 922 38 35 00 | tigaiga.com | €€–€€€)*. The hotel sits in a green oasis surrounded by exotic plants and it has a great view of both Teide and the sea at Puerto de la Cruz. They also offer excellent botanical tours.

Boulders on the mountain are known as "huevos del Teide" (Teide eggs)

THE NORTHEAST

The Cumbre Dorsal mountains separate Tenerife's two coasts like a backbone, climbing towards Mount Teide in the south-west and the largely inaccessible Montañas de Anaga in the northeast. Only two winding roads lead up into this 1,000m-high mountain range.

It's a place of unspoiled landscapes and modern urban life. The capital, Santa Cruz, has merged with the UNESCO-protected La Laguna to form the *Zona Metropolitana*, where almost half of

Montañas de Anaga

Tinerfeños live. Over the last few years, lots of money has been spent sprucing up the two cities. Now they just need a solution to their awful traffic congestion …

Away from the Zona Metropolitana, fertile valleys form Tenerife's "breadbasket" and the biggest wine region in the Canary Islands. Unfortunately, this area has not escaped the impact of mass tourism: large stretches of the coast have been overdeveloped and the valleys have been built up.

OCÉANO
ATLÁNTICO

Punta del Hidalgo
p. 8?

Bajamar
p. 83

Tejina

Tamarco

Teguest

Te

7 Valle de Guerra

TF5

La Lagun

Tacoronte
p. 81

4 El Sauzal

La Costure

La Esperanza

5 La Matanza de Acentejo

28km, 30 mins

Llano c

6 La Victoria de Acentejo

El Tablero

ESPAÑA

3 Cumbre Dorsal ★

Araya

Las Cuevecitas

Candelaria

Malpaís

Arafo

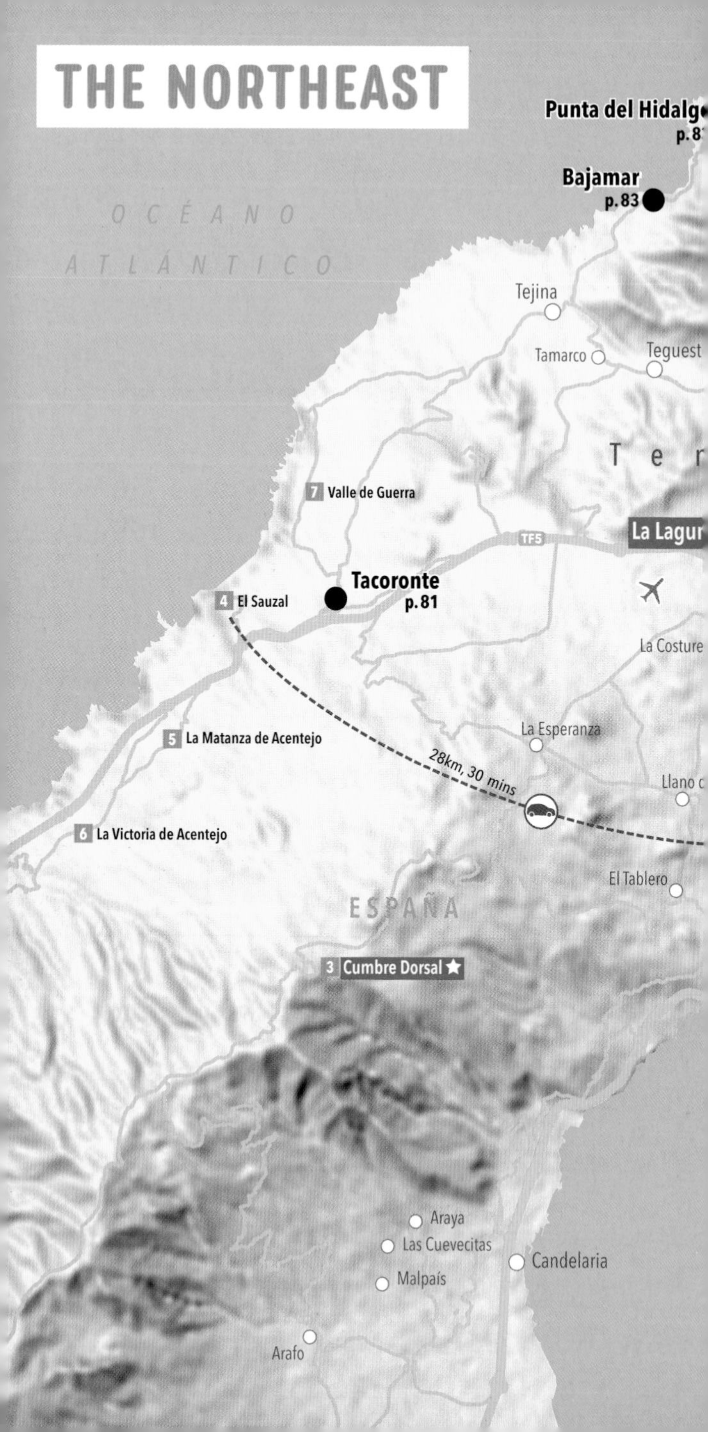

MARCO POLO HIGHLIGHTS

⭐ **SANTA CRUZ DE TENERIFE**
The island's capital has enchanting parks, great art and magnificent music ➤ p. 70

⭐ **TENERIFE ESPACIO DE LAS ARTES**
Santa Cruz's art centre, the TEA, is sensational both inside and out ➤ p. 72

⭐ **PALMETUM**
Palm trees growing on what used to be a landfill site ➤ p. 73

⭐ **AUDITORIO DE TENERIFE**
An architectural masterpiece that has become a symbol of the island ➤ p. 73

⭐ **PLAYA DE LAS TERESITAS**
At weekends this gem of a beach attracts thousands of Tinerfeños ➤ p. 76

⭐ **LA LAGUNA**
Travel back in time to the colonial period at this UNESCO World Heritage Site ➤ p. 76

⭐ **CUMBRE DORSAL**
A tour along the "backbone of Tenerife" will reveal virtually every type of flora on the island ➤ p. 80

⭐ **MONTAÑAS DE ANAGA**
Rugged ridges, gargantuan gorges and isolated inlets ➤ p. 84

SANTA CRUZ DE TENERIFE

Plaza del Príncipe Asturias
Iglesia de San Francisco/ Museo de Bellas Artes
Bodegón el Puntero
Parque García Sanabria
Calle San Lucas
Calle Villalba Hervás
Los Menceyes
Artenerife
Plaza de España
Calle del Castillo
La Rambla
Avenida Ángel Guimerá
Plaza de la Candelaria
Calle del Doctor Allart
La Hierbita
Calle Miraflores
Calle Valentín Sanz
Calle Santo Domingo
Calle de Imeldo Serís
Casa del Carnaval
Paseo la Concordia
Guannabí
Club el Desván
Calle Aguere
C. Afilarmónica Nifú-Nifá
Iglesia de Nuestra Señora de la Concepción
Ausgehviertel la Noria
Calle Fuente de Morales
Mercado de Nuestra Señora de África
Tenerife Espacio de las Artes ★
Avenida de San Sebastián
Afonso
Avenida de San Sebastián
Museo de la Naturaleza y el Hombre
Il Gelato del Mercato
Calle José Manuel Guimerá
los Molinos
Hernández
Navarro
Calle Leoncio Rodríguez
Calle José
Calle Bethencourt y Molina
Avenida La Salle
Calle de Fernández
Aires
Avenida de Buenos
Avenida Tres de Mayo
Avenida Marítima
Dársena Sur
Avenida Tres de Mayo
El Corte Inglés
Calle Álvaro Rodríguez López
Calle Fomento
Avenida Victor Zurita Soler
Avenida de la Constitución
Vía de Servicio Los Llanos
Calle Adán Martín Menis
Palmetum ★
200 m
219 yd
Auditorio de Tenerife ★

SANTA CRUZ DE TENERIFE

(ⅢⅢ M–N 3–4) ★ **Santa Cruz de Tenerife stretches back from the coast towards the jagged mountains on a series of terraces. Plain** apartment blocks and stately colonial buildings harmoniously share the urban space.

Although Santa Cruz (pop. 230,000) is a lively port, the pace never feels hectic. Large parts of the city have been pedestrianised; pavement bars and cafés are firmly in local hands; and Canarian laissez-faire s the order of the day.

The Spaniard Alonso Fernández de Lugo landed in the bay and established the first settlement here in 1494. Santa Cruz was initially overshadowed by La Laguna, 5km inland, but it has been the seat of Tenerife's government since 1723. Commercially important for the city is the sprawling port, where goods from all over the world are traded and where thousands of cruise ship passengers disembark each year.

WHERE TO START

The **bus station (Estación Central de Guaguas)** is just south of the city centre. On your way to the Old Town from here, you will pass the market *(mercado)* and the TEA arts centre. If you are coming by car, try and find a space as close to the **Plaza de España** as possible and set off to explore from there.

SIGHTSEEING

LA RAMBLA

This long boulevard arcs around the centre of the city. Kiosks and benches shaded by tall trees line the pedestrian walkway. Modern sculptures – including ones by Henry Moore and Joan Miró – mix high art into people's daily grind. The old bullring halfway round is now only used for sporting events and pop concerts.

PARQUE GARCÍA SANABRIA

Stroll down wide paths, past enormous trees and exotic flowers. Here and there, you'll run into sculptures, arcades and fountains, with enchanting squares for you sit and catch your breath. You can also get some refreshment at the popular *cafetería* at the (lower) entrance to the park.

IGLESIA DE SAN FRANCISCO/ MUSEO DE BELLAS ARTES 🎏

The Franciscan monks have long since left Santa Cruz and their monastery has been turned into a gallery with works by Dutch and Spanish artists alongside a huge collection of Canarian masters. However, the church still has a religious function. Explore the sacred interior with its volcanic pillars, Baroque altars and carved wood ceilings. *Church: Plaza San Francisco | Museum: Tue–Fri 10am–8pm, Sat, Sun 10am–2pm | admission free | C/ José Murphy 12*

PLAZA DE ESPAÑA & PLAZA DE LA CANDELARIA

The broad *Plaza de España* with its gigantic circular pool of water, numerous trees and floating tropical lamps is very attractive. Its fountain shoots a jet of water skywards every hour. Behind the square, two unassuming pavilions overgrown with plants are home to the tourist information centre and a crafts shop run by Artenerife.

The seat of the island's government administration, *Cabildo Insular*, towers over the other side of the square; an electric nativity scene erected here every year in December attracts many visitors. Near the Cabildo stands the massive memorial to the soldiers who died during the Civil War. Giant athletic warriors carrying swords and helmets – in typical fascist style – commemorate those who fought and died for the dictator Franco.

You can get away from the monstrous sight by (literally) sinking into the ground. ☛ Through an unobtrusive entrance, you can descend into the underground foundations of the *Castillo de San Cristóbal (Mon–Sat 10am–6pm | admission free)*. The fortress was erected in 1575 to fend off pirates and in 1928 – unused for many years – was razed to make room for the expanding city. In the twilight you can see displays on all the city's fortifications. There's even a replica of the famous *El Tigre* cannon, which routed Admiral Nelson in 1797 and now commemorates the military history of the city.

Further inland lies the adjacent *Plaza de la Candelaria*. The "bearer of light" floats on top of a tall, white Carrara marble column – the Virgen de la Candelaria is Tenerife's patron saint. Santa Cruz's shopping district begins at Plaza de la Candelaria, with an eclectic mixture of trendy and traditional shops.

PLAZA DEL PRÍNCIPE ASTURIAS

A magnificent square named after the son of the Spanish king. Mature trees and lush vegetation create the impression of a tropical oasis. Look out for the large

INSIDER TIP
Fishy nickname

bronze fish statue. It is a reminder tha Tinerfeños are often called "little sar dines" *(chicharreros)*.

TENERIFE ESPACIO DE LAS ARTES ⭐

Tenerife's ambitious art and cultural Centre (TEA) is a long building that fits snugly into the *barranco*, the long ravine running through the city towards the coast. Inside, its strictly angled lines, tall glass façades and an open patio allow plenty of light in. A permanent exhibition displays the life's work of the great Tenerife-born surrealist artist Óscar Domínguez. Alongside it are temporary exhibitions of international contemporary art. There is also a large library, a nice cafeteria and 36 internet terminals available free of charge. *Tue–Sun 10am–8pm | admission 5 euros | Av. de San Sebastián 10 | ⏱ 1 hr*

IGLESIA DE NUESTRA SEÑORA DE LA CONCEPCIÓN ☂

The slender steeple of the city's oldest church (1502) was built in typical colonial style and for many years served as an important landmark for sailors. Slim volcanic stone columns support the building internally. Precious Baroque works of art include a high altar, a coloured marble pulpit, paintings, gold and silver treasures and the *Holy Cross of the Conquest* dating from 1494. *Av. Bravo Murillo*

MUSEO DE LA NATURALEZA Y EL HOMBRE ☂

You'll be able to trace the island's history in this magnificent neoclassical former hospital. It starts with Tenerife's volcanic formation and the first plants that established themselves on the barren lava. Next you meet the first settlers, the Guanches, whose preserved skulls are neatly lined up in glass cases. Tools, ornaments and everyday objects belonging to the early Canarian population complete the picture. *Tue–Sun 9am–7pm, Mon 10am-5pm | admission 5 euros | C/ Fuente Morales | museosdetenerife. org| 1 hr*

CASA DEL CARNAVAL

Missed the carnival? No problem! Here, you can slip into a crazy costume before admiring those of queens and drag queens alike. There are also plenty of 3-D videos of carnival in full swing. *Daily 9am-7pm | admission free | C/ Aguere 15 | casacarnavalsanta cruz.com | 30 mins*

PALMETUM ★

A 111-hectare botanical garden has been created where thousands of tonnes of rubbish once quietly rotted away. It contains of palm trees from all over the world. Labyrinthine paths will lead you over little hills, past ponds and waterfalls. Sensitive tropical plants grow in a greenhouse to prepare them for life in the wild. *Daily 10am-6pm, last admission 5pm | admission 6 euros | Av. de la Constitución | palmetumtenerife.es | 1 hr*

AUDITORIO DE TENERIFE ★

The snow-white concert hall is a daring building designed by Spain's star architect, Santiago Calatrava. Its most striking feature is the trio of huge, shell-shaped wings arching over the auditorium, giving the building an airborne, almost weightless appearance. However, it is not only visually

The reading room in Tenerife's Espacio de las Artes is bright and airy

impressive as the acoustics are also extraordinarily good.

Every week concerts in all musical genres, as well as opera and ballet are held in the **INSIDER TIP** *A genre for everyone* bright and airy auditorium. Tours of the building are also available *(4 times a day, book at the ticket desk, by phone 922 56 86 25 or email visitas@auditoriodetenerife.com). Av. de la Constitución | auditoriode tenerife.com*

EATING & DRINKING

BODEGÓN EL PUNTERO
A rustically themed restaurant with all the Canarian classics. The fish here is especially good. *Mon–Sat 12–4.30pm, 8–11pm | C/ San Clemente 3 | tel. 922 28 22 14 | €*

GUANNABÍ
A good spot in the Noria nightlife district. Stone walls with ferns growing down from the ceiling and a mish-mash of furniture make for a relaxed vibe. The food (served on cool plates) is delicious. *Daily from 1pm | C/ Antonio Domínguez Alfonso 34 | tel. 922 87 53 75 | FB: Guannabirestaurante | €€*

IL GELATO DEL MERCATO
Tenerife's best ice cream can be found in the hustle-and-bustle of the market hall. *Tue–Sun 9.30am–3pm | C/ San Sebastián 51 | Mercado de Nuestra Señora de África | €*

LA HIERBITA
The "little herb" serves local classics in the atmospheric surroundings of a historic building in the Old Town. Do as the Spaniards do and order lots of tapas to share. *Closed Sun | C/ Clavel 19 | tel. 922 24 46 17 | lahierbita.com | €-€€*

LOS MENCEYES
Beautifully set tables and high ceilings create an elegance to match the modern Canarian cuisine here while an army of waiters offer excellent, unobtrusive service. One of the best restaurants on the island. *Tapa Negra* next door provides an informal alternative. *Daily | C/ Dr Naveiras 38 | tel. 922 27 67 00 | €€€*

SHOPPING

ARTENERIFE
A low, arching pavilion covered in greenery on the Plaza de España is home to the state-run art and craft chain. *Mon–Fri 10am–2pm and 5–8pm, Sat 10am–2pm | artenerife.com*

EL CORTE INGLÉS ☂
A large department store offering everything from the clothes to fine foods. On the seventh floor there is a panoramic restaurant *(€)*. *Av. Tres de Mayo*

MERCADO DE NUESTRA SEÑORA DE ÁFRICA
Exploring Santa Cruz's Moorish-style town market is an exhilarating experience. In the wide square and in the building's arcades traders sell animals, fruits, vegetables, fish, flowers, cheese and lots more *(daily 7am–3pm | C/ San Sebastián 51)*. On Sundays there's also a flea market.

SPORT & ACTIVITIES

CITY VIEW BUS
Hop on! The orange City View Bus tour starts next to the tourist information on Plaza de España and you can hop off (and then back on) at any of its 15 stops around the city. *Daily 9.30am–6.30pm | 22 euros incl.*

Nuestra Señora de África market is loved by locals and tourists alike

admission to Palmetum | *tenerife cityview.com* | ⏱ *75 mins*

PARQUE MARÍTIMO CÉSAR MANRIQUE

This water park has lots of pools, islands of volcanic rock and plenty of space for sunbathing and makes for a great day out. It was designed by the artist César Manrique. Small cafés serve drinks and snacks. *Daily 10am–6pm| admission 2.50 euros, children 1.50 euros | Av. de la Constitución 5*

NIGHTLIFE

At the weekend, clubbers converge on *La Noria* area at the edge of the Barranco (between the church and the bridge) and then party until the small hours.

CLUB EL DESVÁN

Before and after party: crowds gather inside and out taking in live jazz and art exhibitions. There are other popular evening haunts close by. *Daily from 5.30pm | Pasaje de Sitja 17 | eldesvan-santacruz.com*

LA NORIA NIGHTLIFE AREA

An atmospherically lit network of streets lined with bars and bodegas. Start your night with a relaxed drink at *Bulan*. After that take your pick from the densely packed bars: in *Lagar* there's live music opposite the cool *Mojos y Mojitos* and *Los Reunidos* bars and there's the famous *Marqués de la*

Noria bodega and the *Tasca El Porrón*. *All daily from 8pm | C/ Antonio Domínguez Alfonso*

Santa Cruz's biggest festival is the *Carnaval* which is celebrated to great excess over several weeks (see p. 19).

AROUND SANTA CRUZ DE TENERIFE

🔳 SAN ANDRÉS
10km/10 mins northeast of Santa Cruz on the TF-11

When Santa Cruz's city authorities decided they needed a beach, they headed to this fishing village. However, the volcanic pebbles were not attractive enough, so in 1970 they brought in a few shiploads of fine Saharan sand from what was then the Spanish colony of Western Sahara and thus transformed the village into a resort.

Gleaming brightly in golden yellow, the man-made 1-km-long ★ ✵ *Playa de las Teresitas* is now much enhanced by clusters of palm trees. To prevent the golden sands from being washed away, breakwaters were created. During the week it is often very quiet. But at the weekend Cruzeños flock here in their thousands. Nevertheless, this most Canarian of beaches is still something of a hidden gem among tourists. ▥ *O3*

🔳 GRAN CANARIA
73km/80 mins east of Santa Cruz (on the ferry)

For a day trip to the neighbouring island to the east (for everything you need to know, see MARCO POLO *Gran Canaria*) take the Fred. Olsen Express catamaran from the harbour. This runs several times a day to Agaete and the crossing takes an hour *(return trip from 80 euros per person | tel. 902 10 01 07 | fredolsen.es).* ▥ *0*

LA LAGUNA

(▥ M3) **Do you want to stroll through historic streets, visit ancient monasteries and eat in a rustic bodega? ★ La Laguna,**

a UNESCO World Heritage Site, is great for a day trip – or a longer stay.

But few people want to spend their entire holiday here, because up on the plateau it can get cool and cloudy – the town is often right in the middle of trade wind clouds at an altitude of 500m. What is now a nightmare for holidaymakers was once a blessing for settlers. The cool, moist air ensured bountiful harvests, first for the Guanches, then for the Spanish conquerors. It's not surprising that they made La Laguna the island's first capital in 1496.

It wasn't long before the town had become the archipelago's intellectual centre too. In 1701 the first university in the Canary Islands was founded here. Although in 1723 it lost political

WHERE TO START

Whether you arrive by car, bus or tram, your first stop really ought to be the city's historic centre. The best place to start an exploratory tour of the city is the **Plaza del Adelantado**. This is near the tourist information office where you can book free guided tours of the city *(C/ Obispo Rey Redondo 7 | tel. 922 63 11 94 | turismodelalaguna. com)*. Virtually all the major sights are covered by one 7-euro ticket which can be purchased at any of their ticket desks.

power to the emerging town of Santa Cruz, with its university and an episcopal seat, La Laguna remains the

Sunbathe among the palms and swim in the calm water at Playa de las Teresitas

cultural heart of Tenerife and it continues to be a vibrant city of 156,000 inhabitants. Its colonial legacy is still evident and nurtured, as is reflected in the many fine, typically Canarian buildings.

SIGHTSEEING

MUSEO DE HISTORIA DE TENERIFE 🦐

Even if you're not interested in Canarian history, this palace dating from 1593 is worth a visit. The *Casa de Lercaro (Tue–Sat 9am–8pm, Sun, Mon 10am–5pm | admission 5 euros | C/ San Agustín 22 | museosdetenerife. com)* is a superb example of colonial architecture with its patio's finely carved wooden galleries. In the 🐖 *Fundación Cristino de Vera (admission free)* a few doors further on you can admire nearly 100 paintings by the Tenerife-born painter of the same name. His pointillistic still lifes are slightly morbid – perfect for a holiday meditation on the transience of human life!

> **INSIDER TIP**
> **Art to make you think**

LA CATEDRAL DE LOS REMEDIOS

Tenerife's cathedral was built in the 20th century on the ruins of an older church from 1511. Many works of art are preserved from this time, including expressive sculptures by the Canarian artist José Luján Pérez. The concrete dome completed in 2014 has added a new sense of space and light. *Mon–Fri 10am–8pm, Sat 10am–12.30pm, 2–5pm | admission 5*

euros incl. audio guide | Plaza Fray Albino | lalagunacatedral.com

IGLESIA DE NUESTRA SEÑORA DE LA CONCEPCIÓN

La Laguna's oldest church (1496) has a beautiful painted wooden ceiling, a magnificently carved Baroque pulpit and a baptismal font brought over by the Spanish conqueror Alonso Fernández de Lugo. From the tall bell tower next to the church you can enjoy a fine view of the town and the highlands. *Mon 10am–2pm, Tue–Fri 10am–5pm | C/ Obispo Rey Redondo*

MUSEO DE LA CIENCIA Y EL COSMOS 🦐

You will see the Museum of Science and the Cosmos with its planetarium long before you get there thanks to its huge radio telescope. At over 70 different playful and interactive "stations", you can learn about the connections between the earth, sun, solar system and Milky Way and about human existence in an interactive and fun way. *Tue–Sun 9am–8pm, Sun/Mon 10am–5pm | admission 5 euros | Av. Los Menceyes 70 | museosdetenerife. com| ⏱ 2 hrs*

EATING & DRINKING

EL TIMPLE

Ana is in charge of the kitchen, while her husband Benito alternates between kitchen and dining room. Most Tinerfeños start by ordering one *ración* (portion) – and because Ana's home cooking tastes so good, they can't resist a second one. *Closed Sun,*

Mon | C/ Candilas 4 | tel. 922 25 02 40 | €€

LA BOURMET

The name is a combination of "burger" and "gourmet". They serve more than 10 different burgers, sweet potato fries and home-made bread served with local beers and wines. *Closed Mon | C/ San Agustín 42 | tel. 922 25 04 13 | labourmet.com | €*

LAGUNA NIVARIA

INSIDER TIP
Scintillating snacks and fine dining

The charming bistro in the hotel of the same name is a popular spot for Tinerfeños. If you want something a bit fancier where the finest Canarian ingredients are transformed into creative dishes, head to the main restaurant instead. *Daily 1–4pm and 7–11pm | C/ del Consistorio 13/Plaza del Adelantado 11 | tel. 922 26 42 98 | lagunanivaria.com | €€*

TAPASTÉ

A top spot for vegetarians, vegans and healthy eaters. Everything here is home-made, organic and regional. They don't use preservatives or food colouring, and white sugar is also out. The changing three-course menus cost about 10 euros. *Mon–Sat 1–4pm | Plaza San Cristóbal 37 | tel. 822 01 55 28 | tapaste.es | €*

SHOPPING

The traffic-calmed streets are lined with everything from bric-a-brac to trendy boutiques. *Vinoteca Atlántida*

(San Agustín 55 | FB: Atlántida Artesanía) sell good local wine while *De la Tierra (C/ Obispo Rey Redondo 7)* sells everything from cosmetics to crafts and comestibles.

The huge radio telescope at the Museo de la Ciencia y el Cosmos

NIGHTLIFE

La Laguna is where the island's young people come to party. In C/ Herradores and C/ Obispo Rey Redondo, one bodega follows the next and there are also lots of bars to the south of Plaza del Adelantado towards the university district.

AROUND LA LAGUNA

3 CUMBRE DORSAL ★

10km/10 mins southwest of La Laguna (if driving take the TF-24)

The 42-km road following the narrow mountain ridge from La Laguna to Teide National Park is the most scenic drive on Tenerife. Passing through a kaleidoscope of varied landscapes, the road climbs to a height of 2,300m. To the west of the old capital, cacti and orange trees bask on the arid plateau, at the centre of which is *La Esperanza*, a neat, if rather sleepy, village. *Esperanza Forest* begins higher up. Dense forests and tall eucalyptus trees keep the soil cool, ferns find shade, and laurel and pine plantations will hopefully make up for centuries of deforestation. The rustic *Las Raíces* restaurant *(closed Mon | €)* in the heart of the forest not only serves great food – its setting is like something out of a story book, especially in the fog.

INSIDER TIP
Fairytale pit-stop

From the *Mirador Montaña Grande*, at 1,120m, you can see La Palma on one side, and Gran Canaria on the other. However, your clear views may quickly be enveloped in cloud. Also visible from the *Mirador de Ortuño* is the (sometimes snow-capped) peak of Mount Teide. In summer seven red watchtowers, one of which is visible on the left, are manned around the clock as forest fires are the biggest threat to this region.

The Cumbre Dorsal has amazing views of the Pico del Teide

The Casa del Vino is a wine museum with tasting rooms, tapas bar and restaurant

At 2,000m the road reaches the tree line. The rocks are craggy and only pines, gorse bushes and low shrubs can stand the often-harsh winds and wide temperature fluctuations. Jagged ridges of volcanic rock along with black, leaden and red fields of ash, are evidence of volcanic eruptions that took place millions of years ago. Just past the white towers of the *Observatory*, you will reach the *Centro de Visitantes El Portillo* (see p. 64), the National Park's Information Centre and the start of the lunar landscape surrounding Mount Teide. *G–L 4–6*

TACORONTE

(K3) **As so often on Tenerife, a ring of bland new buildings surrounds the town but in the middle lurks a pretty historical centre.**

For wine connoisseurs, it is definitely worth a visit, because Tacoronte (pop. 22,000) lies at the heart of the largest wine-growing area on the Canary Islands. Extensive vineyards extend along the fertile hillsides. The dozens of *bodegas* will try and tempt you into stopping for a glass.

Look out for signs saying "Guachinche". These are basic bars serving young wine alongside good-value, hearty dishes.

INSIDER TIP
Gourmet pit-stop

SIGHTSEEING

EL CRISTO DE LOS DOLORES

This life-sized statue of Jesus dating from the 17th century stands in the church of a former Augustinian monastery. The triple-naved church contains a wealth of sacred silverwork and its monastery (now a cultural centre) has a lovely cloister. *Daily | Plaza del Cristo*

AROUND TACORONTE

🄴 EL SAUZAL

3km/5 mins southwest of Tacoronte on the TF-215

Most visitors to Tacoronte's neighbouring town (pop. 8,000) head for the *Casa del Vino (Tue 10am–8pm, Wed–Sat 9am–9pm | Sun 10am–6pm | admission 3 euros | casadelvino tenerife.com)*. The "House of Wine" is housed in a 17th-century farmhouse with a lovely view of the sea and of Mount Teide. You'll see historic equipment including wooden presses and much more, documenting the history of wine production on Tenerife. The

INSIDER TIP
Quaff like the locals

cosy Tasca sells great wine by the glass (2 euros per glass) – just like the old days.

The elegant *Casa del Vino* restaurant *(closed Mon | tel. 922 56 38 86 | €€)* serves Canarian classics and has a terrace with a sea view. If you have a car, you can drive 1.5km down to the town centre which "hangs" over the coastal cliffs on several terraces. Behind the ornate 16th-century Iglesia de San Pedro, you'll discover a romantic spot with a *museum (irregular opening hours)* dedicated to Tenerife's unofficial patron saint, Sor María de Jesús. Also lovely is the *Mirador de Garañona* with its view of the surf thundering against the cliffs. *🕮 K3*

🄵 LA MATANZA DE ACENTEJO

5km/7 mins southwest of Tacoronte on the TF-215

A town whose name means the "slaughter of Acentejo" and recalls the momentous battle of 1494 between the Guanches and the Spanish. On that occasion the conquistadors suffered a humiliating defeat. Unfortunately, there's hardly anything old left in La Matanza, which has suffered an epidemic of ugliness. An exception is the 16th-century *La Cuadra de San Diego* estate *(Thu–Sun 1–4pm | Camino Botello 2 | TF-5, exit 23, then TF-217 | tel. 922 57 83 85 | lacuadradesandiego.es | €€)* a pretty restaurant serving creative Canarian cuisine. *🕮 J-K4*

🄶 LA VICTORIA DE ACENTEJO

7km/9 mins southwest of Tacoronte on the TF-215/TF-217

That the Spanish eventually subjugated the Guanches is recalled 2km further on in the name of La Matanza's neighbouring village: La Victoria de Acentejo. Just over a year after the defeat the men returned, but this time with shining armour and an even larger army. The Guanches now had nothing with which to counter them and were finally defeated. To give thanks to God, Captain Fernández de Lugo ordered his men to start work on a church, which was fittingly named *Nuestra Señora de las Victorias*. It stands to this day. *🕮 J4*

🄷 VALLE DE GUERRA

9km/10 mins northeast of Tacoronte on the TF-16

The Valle de Guerra region north of

Punta del Hidalgo

Tacoronte is an important area for wine and fruit and vegetable growing. On the left, just before you enter the town of the same name, is a grand house which holds the *Museo de Antropología de Tenerife* (Tue–Sun 9am–7pm | admission 5 euros | museosdetenerife. com). It's a rather pompous name for a decent museum on everyday life through the ages. ⌘ *K–L2*

BAJAMAR & PUNTA DEL HIDALGO

(⌘ *L–M 1–2*) **Bajamar and Punta del Hidalgo are among the quieter resorts on the island and they are currently undergoing a facelift to make amends for much of 1960s development.**

Bajamar boasts a promenade and two large, free, ☛ *natural swimming pools (Piscinas Naturales)*, which use seawater direct from the ocean. Even if the sea is crashing into the pool's walls, you can carry on calmly swimming your lengths.

INSIDER TIP
Swim safe from the surf

There is also a natural swimming pool in *Punta del Hidalgo*. From there, you can walk about 4km along the coast, past the lighthouse to the "Rock of the Two Brothers" (see p. 84) – two cliffs at the base of the Anaga range. Both places offer great places to stay for those not interested in package tours, etc.

The village of Taganana on the edge of the Anaga mountains

EATING & DRINKING

COFRADÍA DE PESCADORES PUNTA HIDALGO

Go for a swim in the natural pool at *Punta del Hidalgo*, then enjoy some fish in this restaurant run by the fishermen's association – preferably at sunset. *Daily | Av. Marítima 46 | Punta del Hidalgo | tel. 922 15 69 54 | €–€€*

TF-13 coastal road peters out in Punta del Hidalgo. At the end there's an impressive view over the north coast and the *Roque de los Dos Hermanos*, ("Rock of the Two Brothers"). Starting below the bend is a marked hiking trail to *Chinamada*, dramatically situated among the cliffs. Its residents live (as they have for centuries) in whitewashed dwellings carved out of the tufa rock. ⌐ *M1–2*

AROUND BAJAMAR & PUNTA DEL HIDALGO

🟦 CHINAMADA
9km/3.5 hrs east of Punta del Hidalgo (follow the marked paths on foot PR-TF 10)

MONTAÑAS DE ANAGA

(⌐ *L–M 1–2*) **Northeast of Santa Cruz and La Laguna, increasingly windy roads climb up into the cool** ★ **Anaga Mountains. For millions of years a laurel forest has survived in this remote area, where there is still very little human habitation.**

These steep inclines were out of reach even for the Spanish settlers, who from the outset indiscriminately felled the island's forests. In many places the woodland is interspersed with bizarre heather trees, from whose branches hang long strands of lichen. Like sponges they absorb moisture from the trade wind clouds, which ascend in dense swathes. If the mist clears, the *miradores* (viewing points) afford fantastic long-distance views. The sweeping panorama from the highest, *Pico del Inglés* (992m), takes in the Atlantic surf at Punta del Hidalgo and the beach at Las Teresitas. At the Mirador Cruz del Carmen, marked footpaths wind through rugged mountain terrain. The *visitor centre (daily 9.30am–4pm)* has leaflets detailing the footpaths. Try the Camino de los Sentidos, a picturesque one-hour

INSIDER TIP
A walk to awaken the senses

circular walk through the "enchanted forest". You can regain your strength with dishes made using regional ingredients at *La Gangochera (daily | tel. 922 26 42 12 | FB: Gangochera | €)* opposite the visitor centre.

The biggest village in these mountains is *Taganana (▢ N2)* which sits at the foot of a broad valley under high peaks. There is a stunning Flemish-style altarpiece in *Nuestra Señora de las Nieves*, a church built in 1506. Down on the coast, the fishermen's hamlets of *Roques de la Bodega* and *Benijo* face the wrath of the waves. If you stay up at the top, you will get to *Mirador El Bailadero*, which has a stunning view of the steep cliffs on this stretch of coast.

WHERE TO STAY

CITY STYLE OR SEASIDE VIEWS

Enjoying a scenic location on the edge of Santa Cruz's main park, the architecture at the *Grand Mencey (293 rooms | Av. Dr José Naveiras 38 | tel. 922 60 99 00 | grandhotelmencey.com | €€€)* harks back to the medieval era while its stripped back, white interior is radically modern.

The *Jardín de la Paz (11 apartments | C/ Acentejo | La Matanza | tel. 922 57 83 19 | jardin-de-la-paz.com | €€€)* is totally different. It "floats" above a cliff with amazing views and a sensational breakfast served in a bright tropical garden.

THE SOUTHEAST

SEMI-DESERT BETWEEN MOUNTAINS & COAST

There are few hidden charms in this region. Arid land, over-developed resorts and a handful of sleepy towns. And it can get very dusty – and gusty – with trade winds casting a veil over the sun. There are some gems here, though, like Candelaria, a place of pilgrimage on the coast, and El Médano, whose natural beaches are the island's biggest.

Once you get a bit higher, it gets prettier. There are endless strings of pumice stone walls criss-crossing between terraced fields where

The Basílica is the symbol of Candelaria

fruit, vegetables are grown. Lots of wine is produced here and the pastures are home to goats and sheep whose milk is used to make excellent cheese.

The drive along winding TF-28 highway from Los Cristianos to Santa Cruz de Tenerife is worthwhile. There are many fine views en route and traditional villages where little has changed even with the arrival of mass tourism.

THE SOUTHEAST

ESPAÑA

Tenerife

52km 1 hr 10 mins

Paisaje Lunar ★

Arico V

4 Arico

Villa de Arico

La Cisnera

Vilaflor
p.96

El Río

24km · 25 mins

6 Granadilla

San Migu
de Tajao

San Miguel de Abona

San Isidro

7 Iter

Parque De La Reina

Aeropuerto
Reina Sofía

Arenas del Mar

TF1

El Médano ★
p.93

Playa Médano

5 Los Abrigos

Playa de la Tejita

Urbanización El Guincho

Las Cuevecitas
Araya
Malpaís

Virgen de Candelaria ★

● **Candelaria**
p. 90

1 Arafo

TF1

◉ **Pirámides de Güímar ★**
● **Güímar**
p. 91

2 El Puertito de Güímar

8km, 10 mins

○ El Escobonal

Fasnia

3 Porís de Abona

7km, 10 mins

MARCO POLO HIGHLIGHTS

★ VIRGEN DE CANDELARIA
The holiest of holies on the Canaries:
Tenerife's Madonna ➤ p.90

★ PIRÁMIDES DE GÜÍMAR
Mysterious stone pyramids and a ship
made of reeds ➤ p.91

★ EL MÉDANO
A mecca for windsurfing and popular
with a younger crowd ➤ p. 93

★ PAISAJE LUNAR
A "lunar landscape" made from volcanic
rock ➤ p. 97

OCÉANO

ATLÁNTICO

4 km
2.49 mi

CANDELARIA

(□ L5–6) **In this small town of 20,000 inhabitants, everything revolves around the *Virgen de Candelaria*, Tenerife's patron saint.**

A huge pilgrimage is celebrated in her honour every August, and a steady stream of pilgrims arrives here all year round. Take a stroll through the Old Town with its occasionally steep lanes, small shops and the broad square that opens up towards the ocean.

SIGHTSEEING

BASÍLICA DE CANDELARIA

The triple-naved basilica built in 1959 in a slightly exaggerated Canarian neo-colonial style is home to the archipelago's most revered shrine, the ★ *Virgen de Candelaria*. The extravagantly clad Virgin, adorned with crown and jewels, occupies the place of honour in a gold-framed, illuminated chamber above the altar. A modern mural tells the story behind the statue. Guanche shepherds found a statue of the Virgin Mary on the beach, which they immediately declared their "magical mother". She repaid their faith by performing miracles (which continue to this day). Today's Madonna was made in 1827 by local artist, Fernando Estévez, after the original was lost during a storm.

PLAZA DE LA PATRONA DE CANARIAS

The vast square in front of the cathedral was built for the throngs of pilgrims who come every year in mid-August to pay homage to the Virgen de Candelaria. Nine rather strange, oversized *bronze statues* sit prominently on the waterfront. They were created in 1993 by Canarian artist, José Abad, and depict the *menceys*, who ruled over Tenerife at the time of the Spanish conquest. The Guanche kings are dressed in animal skins and hold spears, sticks and mallets. With their clean-shaven faces, athletic bodies and flowing hair, they embody the ideal of the "noble savage".

Beyond the statues there is a dark sandy beach which stretches 800m to the north. If you follow the promenade to the south, you will get to the impressive *Cueva de San Blas*, which is 14m long and over 5m high. This is where the shepherds are said to have found the statue of the Virgin Mary in the 14th century, and so the chapel was built on the site. However, recent archaeology has shown the caves here have served ritual purposes for at least 2,000 years.

Hungry? Head back to the Plaza de La Patrona, where *Plaza (daily | tel. 922 50 41 31 | €€)* serves homely Canarian cuisine. After a good lunch, you may feel up to tackling the town's steep roads. The small steeple which protrudes out of the jumble of houses is the baroque *Iglesia de Santa Ana* (1575).

SHOPPING

MERCADILLO

Three times a week a small market is held at the entrance to the road leading to the Plaza de la Patrona de Canarias. At the weekend you will find crafts, knick-knacks and religious objects on sale; on Wednesdays farmers from the surrounding area come into Candelaria to sell fresh produce. *Wed, Sat 9am–2pm*

GÜÍMAR

(▥ K6) **Many people have heard of the Pyramids of Güímar, but few know the town (pop. 19,000) itself. The small Old Town with its churches and large houses is testament to its one-time wealth. Vineyards in the surrounding Valle de Güímar provide much-needed greenery in this dry region.**

SIGHTSEEING

IGLESIA SAN PEDRO APÓSTOL

The church, built in 1610, boasts wooden ceilings, a carved pulpit and grand circular altarpieces. The trompe l'oeil painting behind the altar appears to lengthen the nave. *Plaza San Pedro*

PIRÁMIDES DE GÜÍMAR ★ ⚑

Spread over a large expanse of land to the north of the town are six stone pyramids. In the past, farmers dried their fruit and vegetables on the steps here and did not even think about the strange architecture. Why should they? The eastern part of the island was criss-crossed by stone walls and every generation added new ones. It needed an outsider to take a closer

These statues in Candelaria commemorate the old rulers of Tenerife

A boat made of reeds that crossed the Atlantic: Thor Heyerdahl's *Ra II*

look at these "piles of stones" to discover their symmetrical beauty. Having studied the alignment of the pyramids and carried out a survey of their exact location, the Norwegian anthropologist Thor Heyerdahl concluded that they were probably used for sacred rituals and for astronomic observation. He also believed they formed a transatlantic link between ancient Egyptian pyramids and those of the Maya in Central America.

An *ethnographic park* (daily 9.30am–6pm | admission 11 euros | C/ Chacona | piramidesdeguimar.es) excellently explains these theories and casts new light on life for the Canary Islands' first settlers. Heyerdahl's work is covered in one section of the park which contains a life-size recreation of the *Ra II*, the 12-m-long ship, built entirely of reeds, on which he crossed the Atlantic from Morocco to Barbados in 1970.

The *Tropicarium* is also well worth visiting. Carnivorous and poisonous plants are allowed to thrive in this small garden. Did you know that oleander plants and birds of paradise flowers are toxic?

EATING & DRINKING

CASONA SANTO DOMINGO

This town house dates from the 16th century and serves traditional food alongside good Canarian wines. C/ Santo Domingo 32 | tel. 922 51 02 29 | casonasanto domingo.com | €€

FINCA SALAMANCA

This historic manor house lies in the middle of the grounds of an avocado finca which serves excellent food. The dining room is in the old grain store and everything from duck to tuna carpaccio tastes excellent. *Daily | Ctra Güímar–El Puertito, Km1.5 | tel. 922 51 45 30 | hotel-fincasalamanca.com | €€*

INSIDER TIP — Granary dining

AROUND GÜÍMAR

1 ARAFO
4km/5 mins north of Güímar on the TF-523

This untouristy village (pop. 5,000) 4km north of Güímar is a gem, with a laurel-shaded plaza and a small bar *(daily | €)*. ⊞ K6

2 EL PUERTITO DE GÜÍMAR
5 km/10 mins east of Güímar on the TF-612

There may not be a beach but you can still swim! 4km east of Güímar in the harbour of El Puertito, ladders allow you access to the water. There is also a small promenade with al fresco bars and restaurants where you can pick up a cool drink or some basic food. ⊞ L7

3 PORÍS DE ABONA
18km/20 mins south of Güímar on the TF-61/TF-1

Just 2,000 people live in this fishing village with its winding harbour promenade and good swimming beach. The view of the bay and delicious tapas at *Café al Mar (daily | mobile tel. 636 94 38 20 | €)* make the detour to Poris worthwhile. ⊞ K9

4 ARICO
35 km/1 hr south of Güímar on the TF-28

This village (pop. 7,000) is made up of several sections which stretch along the main road. At *Arico Nuevo*, a Site of Special Historical Architectural Interest, beautifully preserved village houses line both sides of a sloping side road and there's a quiet plaza with chapel. It's all neatly whitewashed and the doors and window frames are painted in classic Canarian green – something of a rarity for Tenerife. ⊞ J9

EL MÉDANO

(⊞ H11) ★ **El Médano ("The Dune"), is located 7km east of Reina Sofía airport and is home to Tenerife's longest natural beaches. The bright sand stretches for miles along the coast and is popular with bathers and surfers alike. The latter love the strong winds here, which can put off more sedate holidaymakers …**

The village itself has a population of 3,000 and is extremely laid back – this is still a place where the locals rule the roost over tourists. The broad Plaza Príncipe de Asturias is a place where old Canarians and young northern

Montaña Roja, "Red Mountain", rises above Playa de la Tejita

Europeans can chat over a beer. There is good fish to be had too – fresh off the boats.

EATING & DRINKING

CABALLO BLANCO

How does tuna cannelloni with goat's cheese sound? The "White Horse" serves its experimental fish dishes on a terrace over the sea. *Closed Fri | Paseo El Picacho 8 | FB: El Caballo Blanco | €€*

SPORT & ACTIVITIES

Quite a few surf schools have taken up residence in El Médano. *Tenerife Kitesurf Center (Paseo Ntra. Sra. de las Mercedes de Roja 58 | tel. 666 20 11 60 | tenerifekitesurf.es)* offers a full range of outdoor activities. Whether you'd like to lift off on a kitesurf or quietly paddle about on a SUP, they will have something for you.

BEACHES

Playa Médano begins in the middle of the resort and is just over 2km long. Swimmers splash about near the shore — but be careful because the wind occasionally brings kitesurfers uncomfortably close to the beach. Behind the beach is a volcano, the Montaña Roja, and beyond it the sandy *Playa de la Tejita* – a popular nudist spot – stretches towards Los Abrigos. To the north of El Médano there are rocky beaches at *Playa del Cabezo* and *Playa de la Jaquita*, which are popular with surfers (international surfing competitions are held here).

restaurants with beautiful sea views. Small and fairly basic, they serve excellent, simply prepared seafood literally fresh off the boats! The best sea view is from the narrow terrace of the *Perlas del Mar (closed Mon | tel. 922 17 00 14 | €€)*, at the tip of the small cape. Watch the boats sailing in and out while enjoying a plate of fresh fish, potatoes and *mojo* sauce. A small market is held every Tuesday from 6pm to 9pm. *⚏ G12*

6 GRANADILLA

11.5km/10 mins north of El Médano on the TF-64

The centre of this little town set back from the coast has retained its old-school charm. The erstwhile *Convento de San Francisco* is today a cultural centre *(closed Sat and Sun | Centro de Cultura | Plaza González Mena)*. The old post office, next to the baroque church of San Antonio de Padua, is now a smart hotel. *⚏ H11*

7 ITER

7km/5 mins east of El Médano on the TF-1

The *Instituto Tecnológico de Energías Renovables* (Institute for Renweable Energy) has an outdoor exhibition that explains solar, wind and geothermal energy. There are also 24 futuristic zero-carbon houses designed by architects from all over the world, who

> **INSIDER TIP**
> Construction with a clear conscience

have managed to blend beautiful design with environmental innovation. Electricity comes from the wind and the sun, and water is produced in

NIGHTLIFE

Surfers head to the bars (such as *Flashpoint*) on the Plaza and on the promenade when they need to quench their thirst.

AROUND EL MÉDANO

5 LOS ABRIGOS

6km/6 mins west of El Médano on the TF-643

Sadly, this village (pop. 2,000) is scarred by ugly tower blocks. However, if you get down to the harbour, you will understand why tourists from all over the south flock here every day. Lining the promenade are several

Paisaje Lunar: Canarian lunar landscape

the centre's own desalination plant. The design of the houses varies enormously: light sun-catching cubes are next to bunkers dug into the earth, and playful curves contrast with hard angles. You can stay in the houses but you will need a car (and earplugs!) *Polígono Industrial de Granadilla | tel. 922 74 77 00 | casas.iter.es | €€ | ⊞ H–J11*

VILAFLOR

(⊞ F9) **If you drive into the national park from the south, you'll pass through this somewhat sleepy village (pop. 3,000).**

Vilaflor, among the highest municipalities in Spain, stands at 1,400m above sea level, and is surrounded by terraced fields, where local farmers cultivate vines and vegetables. One small business bottles spring water under the brand names of *Pinalito* and *Fuente Alta*, which is drunk everywhere on Tenerife. Some women here still top up their income by making traditional *rosetas*, delicate lace rosettes, which are sewn on to blankets and shawls. You can find the lace on sale in the souvenir shops on the church square, where the women will happily demonstrate their extremely time-consuming art.

Life in Vilaflor is far from the bustle of the resorts and the dusty coastline

Another local curiosity is the ★ *Paisaje lunar (▥ G8)*, 20km northeast of Vilaflor. This "lunar landscape" is a bizarre volcanic formation unique to the Canaries. You can only get there on foot (the PR-TF trail) either from Vilaflor's church square (13km/5 hrs there and back) or on a slightly longer route departing from Km66 of the TF-21.

EATING & DRINKING

RINCÓN DEL ROBERTO

Perfect if it is cool outside! A hearth and hearty food will soon warm you up. Señora Araceli and her husband Jesús prepare Canarian classics (try the rabbit and goat) accompanied by local wine. *Closed Tue | Av. Hermano Pedro 27 | tel. 922 70 90 35 | €€*

and you can breathe in the fresh mountain air of the Mount Teide region. The small, 16th-century *Iglesia de San Pedro Apóstol* dominates the town's central square. The *Casa de los Soler* façade on the church is testimony to the power once held by the noble family who founded the town.

The area just above the town is known for its Canary pine forests. ▸ One famous example of the species is the 60m Pino Gordo; it is said that you will be lucky in love if you hug it. It's by the TF-21 road that winds its way up to Mount Teide, passing some stunning viewpoints on the way.

DER TIP
Tree-mendous height

WHERE TO STAY

NATURE RESORT

A truly Canarian experience. The ochre buildings of the *San Blas Nature Resort (331 rooms | Av. Greñamora 1 | Los Abrigos | tel. 922 74 90 10 | sandos.com | €€–€€€)* blend perfectly with the island's volcanic rock, while the inside pays tribute to Tenerife's amazing flora. The hotel has a visitor centre that allows you access to a nature reserve where you can learn more about the island's geology and nature as you head up a wild gorge and across a beautiful lake.

THE SOUTHWEST

TOTAL TOURISM

Most tourists think of the southwest when they think of Tenerife. This is where you'll find the finest beaches and where sunshine is practically guaranteed. Infrastructure here has developed to meet the needs of package tourism: hotels range from affordable to super-luxury, and there are shopping centres, restaurants from around the world, and more water sports and golf courses than anyone could possibly want.

The resort of Los Gigantes is named after the gigantic cliffs

You can walk through dramatic ravines or take a boat trip to look for whales or to head over to La Gomera – Tenerife's "little sister".

The change here has been so rapid that it has effectively wiped out traditional life. Farms have been sold and their fields lie fallow. The south has got rich off tourism and many locals live from it – indeed in this dry region there is almost no alternative.

THE SOUTHWEST

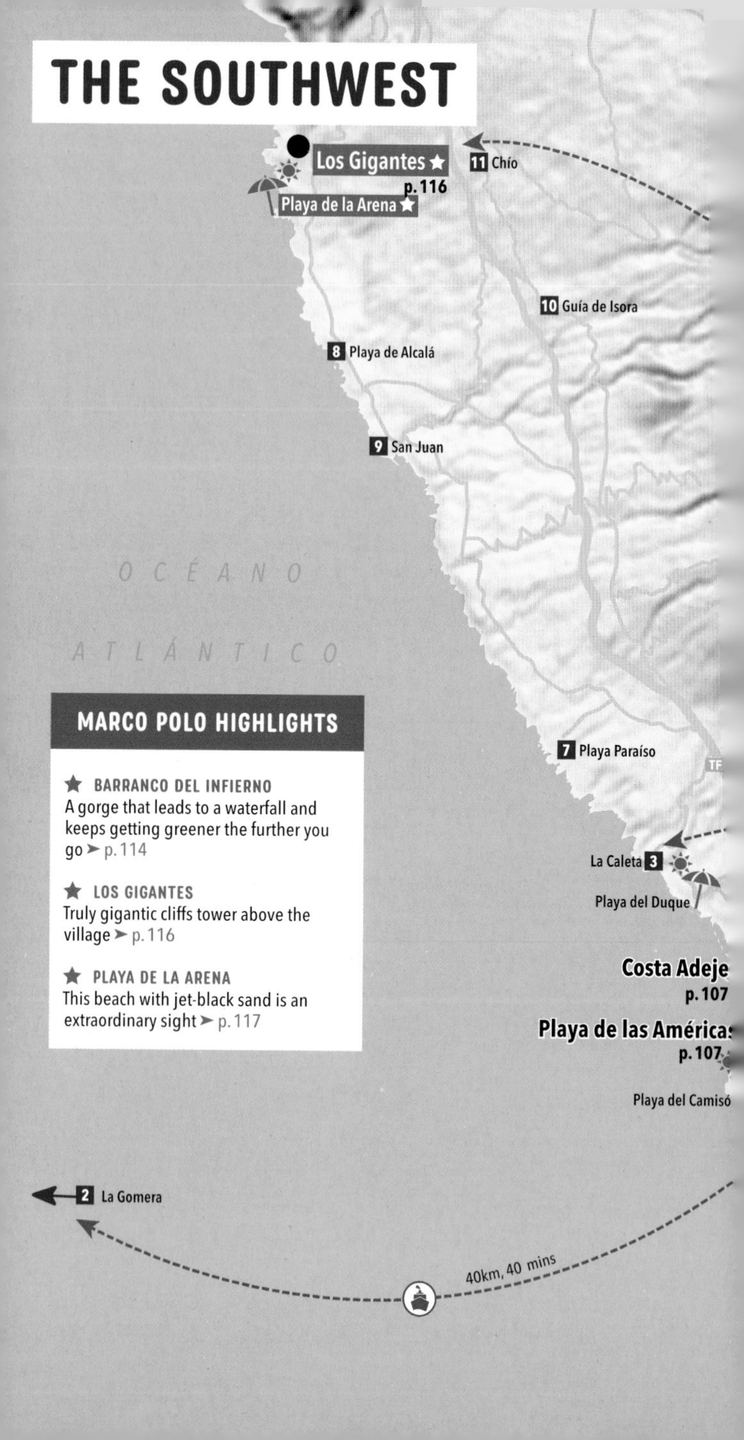

Los Gigantes ★
p. 116
Playa de la Arena ★

11 Chío

10 Guía de Isora

8 Playa de Alcalá

9 San Juan

OCÉANO

ATLÁNTICO

7 Playa Paraíso

TF

La Caleta **3**

Playa del Duque

Costa Adeje
p. 107

Playa de las Américas
p. 107

Playa del Camisó

MARCO POLO HIGHLIGHTS

★ **BARRANCO DEL INFIERNO**
A gorge that leads to a waterfall and keeps getting greener the further you go ➤ p. 114

★ **LOS GIGANTES**
Truly gigantic cliffs tower above the village ➤ p. 116

★ **PLAYA DE LA ARENA**
This beach with jet-black sand is an extraordinary sight ➤ p. 117

2 La Gomera

40km, 40 mins

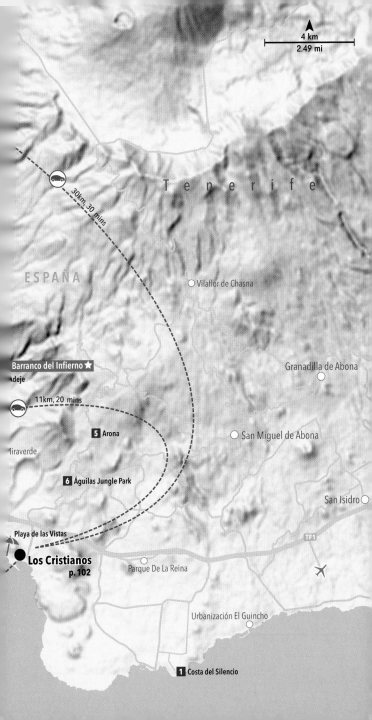

4 km
2.49 mi

Tenerife

ESPAÑA

30km, 30 mins

Vilaflor de Chasna

Granadilla de Abona

Barranco del Infierno ★

Adeje

11km, 20 mins

San Miguel de Abona

5 Arona

Miraverde

San Isidro

6 Águilas Jungle Park

TF1

Playa de las Vistas

Parque De La Reina

Los Cristianos
p. 102

Urbanización El Guincho

1 Costa del Silencio

LOS CRISTIANOS

(□ E11) **At first sight Los Cristianos, the oldest resort in the south, is pretty depressing: ugly hotels, terrible traffic and hardly any trees. However, the local council has pulled the emergency brakes and started to give the place a facelift. Traffic-calming schemes have been implemented, roads have been lined with palms and promenades smartened up, much to the delight of the many holidaymakers who enjoy coming to Los Cristianos because it still has local life.**

It has also become popular for people with disabilities because the beaches, restaurants and infrastructure have been adapted for a wide range of needs. The *Spa & Sport Mar y Sol* is the only completely wheelchair-accessible resort on the Canaries.

The beach promenade links the new and old parts of the town. The beach teems with swimmers, further out in the bay fishing boats and ferries come in and out of their docks. Walkers almost unwittingly end up in the part of the town above the harbour, which, with its narrow alleys and tiny courtyards, serves as a reminder that the now-bustling seaside resort was once a quiet village.

EATING & DRINKING

CASA TAGORO
Far and wide the best food. Enjoy a special evening in this restaurant decorated with antique furniture where the German chef Gerhard Brodträger creates dishes inspired by both his Atlantic home and his alpine heritage. A wide variety of tapas are served and the tasting menus are highly recommended. It is slightly hidden behind the Reverón Plaza hotel. *Tue–Sat 6–11pm, Sun 1–11pm | C/ Valle de Menéndez 28 | tel. 822 66 08 33 | casatagoro.com | €€–€€€*

INSIDER TIP
The Atlantic meets the Alps

EL CINE
One of the town's oldest restaurants tucked away in a small alley close to the promenade. It serves simple, authentic food, as it always has. Choice is limited which means everything is fresh. That said, the traditional wrinkly potatoes *(papas arrugadas)* with *mojo* sauce are always on the menu. *Closed Mon | C/ Juan Bariajo 8 | mobile tel. 609 10 77 58 | €–€€*

LA FORTUNA NOVA
The sumptuous three-course set menus in *La Fortuna Nova (closed Sun | Av. del Valle Menéndez | tel. 922 79 51 92)* cost just 8 euros for lunch (a little more in the evening) and can be enjoyed on the shady terrace or in the quaint dining room. Unbeatable value for money. *Closed Sun | C/ del Valle Menéndez 16 | tel. 922 79 51 92 | €*

The marina at Los Cristianos with the mountains behind

MESÓN CASTELLANO

More Castilian than Canarian: you sit, surrounded by hunting trophies, lots of wood and wrought-iron chandeliers, while Señor Manuel José serves excellent meat dishes, often barbecued, plus wine from the mainland. *Closed Tue | C/ Alfonso Domínguez 40 | El Camisón | tel. 922 79 63 09 | mesoncastellano.com | €€*

PICCOLO

As the name suggests, it's all about antipasti, Roman-style pasta and daily Italian specials – on a terrace overlooking the sea above Playa de las Vistas. *Daily from 1pm | Av. Habana 11 | tel. 922 79 67 88 | FB: piccolo tenerife | €€*

SHOPPING

LA ALPIZPA

Canarian crafts produced by people with disabilities are on sale at this stall on the *Playa de los Cristianos* promenade. *Mon–Sat 10am–1pm and 5–8.30pm*

LIBRERÍA BARBARA

Bookshop with new and second-hand titles in lots of languages, plus maps and guidebooks. Run by a mother and daughter team. *Mon–Fri 10am–1.30pm and 4–8pm, Sat 10am–1.30pm | C/ Juan Pablo Abril 6 | libreriabarbara.com*

MERCADILLO

At the popular Sunday flea market (rastro) between Arona Gran Hotel and the beach, you'll find a lot of kitsch counterfeit objects, but also occasionally beautiful craftwork. *Sun 9am–2pm*

SPORT & ACTIVITIES

Here in the south virtually every sport imaginable is on offer: squash, golf and mini-golf, trampolining, parachute jumping, hang-gliding, hiking, cycling, climbing, sailing, windsurfing, jet skiing, scuba diving, deep-sea fishing and much more.

To find out what exactly is on offer, take a walk along the beach, around the harbours and in the shopping malls and talk to the various agencies or pick their leaflets up in the tourist information office.

BOAT TRIPS

A gently rocking boat, the sea breeze and the possibility of spotting dolphins? Tourist boats set sail from the harbour every day when the sea is calm. There are more than 25 species of whale and dolphin off Tenerife's coast and the chances of spotting them on a whale-watching tour are good, with pilot whales and porpoises being the most common. Information and tickets are available at the end of the promenade just by the harbour. *Mar de Ons | tel. 922 75 15 76 | mardeons-tenerife.com*

INSIDER TIP
Find Flipper!

CAMEL PARK 🐫

Camel rides are available from *La Camella*, an inland village. *Daily 10am–3.30pm | rides (20 mins) cost 22 euros per person, children 11 euros | getting there: TF-51 3.5km (free buses from the south) | tel. 922 72 11 21 | camelpark.es*

GOLF

Take your pick from five courses. The green fee for 18 holes is approx. 60 euros in the summer and about double that in the winter. The *Amarilla Golf & Country Club (getting there: Autopista del Sur, Los Abrigos exit, Km3 | tel. 922 73 03 19 | amarillagolf. es)* has 18 holes, a nine-hole course and a putting course, plus riding stables, tennis courts and swimming pools.

Golf del Sur (getting there: Autopista del Sur, Los Abrigos exit, Km4 | tel. 922 73 81 70 | golfdelsur.es) has 27 holes, plus a golf academy.

Golf Center Los Palos (getting there: Autopista del Sur, Guaza exit, Km1.5 | *tel. 922 16 90 80 | golflospalos.com)* is an attractive nine-hole course offering golf classes for players at all levels.

BEACHES

Everything you need: all the beaches here have showers, toilets and first-aid stations.

PLAYA DE LOS CRISTIANOS

Great for volleyball, pedalos and sunbathing. This broad 1-km-long beach starts right next to the harbour, meaning the water might not necessarily be clean. The area to the south of Los Cristianos is popular with nudists.

There are plenty of options for water-sports fans

Bahía del Duque, a posh resort on the Costa Adeje

PLAYA DE LAS VISTAS

This bright and broad beach is protected by breakwaters meaning you can almost always swim here. There is an eye-catching fountain set against the green backdrop of the promenade. Wooden planks take you down to the water and there are lots of lifeguards around (who also help disabled people swim).

NIGHTLIFE

What nightlife there is is concentrated around the promenade. Just off the *Playa de las Vistas* (enter from Av. de Habana), there are a number of cocktail bars. The best is *Agua de Coco* where they make excellent mojitos with a sea view.

FESTIVALS & EVENTS

There is hardly a month without a festival in Los Cristianos and the Arona area. It starts with *Carnaval* in February/March, followed by *Arona Fashion Week* in May, the modern *ARN Culture Pride* in June and the more traditional boat processions to honour Carmen, the patron saint, at the start of September.

There are small folk festivals in the winter at the weekend, when musicians and dancers parade along the promenade.

AROUND LOS CRISTIANOS

1 COSTA DEL SILENCIO

12km/10 mins from Los Cristianos on the TF-655/TF-66

"Coast of Silence" – this is not the most fitting name for the southernmost point of Tenerife. Planes land at the nearby airport almost every minute during the high season. And the landscape beyond the town isn't particularly attractive: banana plantations behind high walls and expanses of plastic sheeting protecting the fields of vegetables don't exactly scream beauty.

The former fishing port of Las Galletas still has a small promenade with fish restaurants, such as the basic *La Marina (daily | €–€€)* and the smarter *Le Grand Bleu (daily | €–€€)* ⌑ *F12*

2 LA GOMERA

40km/40 mins west of Los Cristianos (by ferry)

Several times a day the *Fred Olsen Express* hydrofoil *(return from 68 euros per person | tel. 902 10 01 07 | fredolsen.es)* whisks passengers from Los Cristianos harbour across to the neighbouring island of La Gomera (journey time approx. 40 mins) – a great spot for a day trip. A slightly cheaper alternative is the slower ferry operated by the *Naviera Armas* shipping company *(tel. 902 45 65 00 | navieraarmas.es)*. ⌑ *0*

PLAYA DE LAS AMÉRICAS/ COSTA ADEJE

(⌑ E11) **The northern edge of Los Cristianos seamlessly merges into the tourist citadel of *Playa de las Américas*, which in turn becomes the smarter *Costa Adeje* and *Bahía del Duque* resorts further north. A set of great beaches, protected by breakwaters come "with all the trimmings", making this a great place for a holiday.**

Beyond the promenade are the hotels, apartment complexes, shopping malls (with travel agencies) and restaurants whose northern European cuisine will have you feeling right at home … But don't worry, there are a couple of Spanish restaurants too. While Playa de las Américas has seen better days, Costa Adeje, and even more so Bahía del Duque, is calmer and prettier. The elegant hotels there court a wealthy clientele, but their beaches are open to the public. You can take whale-watching trips (among others) from the yacht harbour at Puerto Colón.

SIGHTSEEING

PASEO MARÍTIMO

There are virtually no traditional tourist sights here but a walk along the pleasantly shady promenade is a decent substitute. It runs for 12km along the coast. You can get all the

PLAYA DE LAS AMÉRICAS

Casino Playa de las Américas
La Casita de Taby
Playa del Duque
Avenida de los Pueblos
Magma
Avenida Quinto Centenario
Playa de Troya
Avenida
El Gomero
Papagayo Beach Club
Rafael
Siam Mall
Puig Lluvina
Playa de las Américas
Avenida Santiago Puig
Lluvina
Calle Noelia Afonso Cabrera
Sugar & Spices
Puig
Cuesta
Gómez
Arquitecto
Avenida
Rafael
Avenida
Antonio
Domínguez
Av. Las Américas
Artenerife
Pirámide de Arona
Playa del Camisón
Friends Lounge Bar

400 m
437 yd

TOURIST TRAIN

Had enough of walking? The tourist train will take you on a tour through the streets of Los Cristianos and Playa de las Américas. *Daily 10am–10pm | 10 euros, kids half price | departure: corner of Av. R Puig Lluvina/ Av. Santiago Puig*

EATING & DRINKING

EL GOMERO

A simple, rustic restaurant serving a wide range of good Canarian dishes including squid, paella and gofio mousse for pudding – all at very affordable prices. 🐷 Also does good-value lunch menus. *Closed Sun | Av. V Centenario 1 | tel. 922 75 07 13 | €-€€*

INSIDER TIP
Canarian fast food

FRIENDS LOUNGE BAR

The name says it all: casual, informal atmosphere on the beach promenade with friendly service and simple dishes. You're welcome to stop by even if it's just for a drink. *Daily | Paseo Tarajal | CC Compostela Beach | tel. 922 78 94 66 | friendstenerife.com | €-€€*

LA CASITA DE TABY

This little tapas bar is hidden away in an ugly shopping mall. The passionate owners serve up a wide selection of Spanish home cooking – from potato salad to cheese and *jamón* platters and squid. Atmospheric in the evening with the artfully lit promenade. *Daily | Av. Puig Lluvina | CC Salytien | tel. 651 98 87 57 | €*

way to La Caleta on foot … if you want! One particularly attractive building on the promenade is *Arts Lifestyle & Shopping (Francisco Andrade Fumero 1 | artstenerife.com)*, which sits majestically on a small cape. With lots of sculptures and installations, it is like walking through a sculpture park.

PAPAGAYO BEACH CLUB

Excellent location on the promenade under palm trees with the sound of waves crashing in the background. Glistening white interior design with a wide choice of cocktails and snacks served all day long. DJ sessions and live flamenco organised in the evenings several times a week. *Daily 10am–3am, weekends until 6am | Paseo Marítimo/ Av. Rafael Puig Lluvina | on the border with Costa Adeje | tel. 922 78 89 16 | papagayo beachclub.com | €*

SUGAR & SPICES

This fashionable, black and white themed restaurant mainly serves pizza and pasta. Popular choices include pappardelle with wild mushrooms, gnochetti in a white wine sauce and tortellini with spinach. The highlight though is the "Diana" perch, garnished with mussels and prawns. *Daily | Av. Rafael Puig Llavina | Village Club | tel. 922 79 22 71 | FB: sugar spicestenerife | €€*

SHOPPING

There are plenty of malls *(centros comerciales* or *CC)* with outlets selling everything from kitschy keepsakes to tasty edible souvenirs.

Playa de las Américas' promenade

ARTENERIFE

The state-run handicrafts chain has a stall at Playa de Troya that looks like the sawn-off hull of a ship. You're guaranteed to find Canarian products here and each item is unique. *Mon–Fri 10am–8.30pm Sat 10am–1pm | Av. del Litoral. There is another Artenerife shop at the western end of Playa de las Vistas*

SIAM MALL 🚿

A free bus will take you to the beautiful and exotically stylish shopping mall next to Siam Park. You'll find more here than just the normal brand names (Mango, Zara etc.); there are also fine local retailers. Park your kids in the playground and your car in the free car park. *Daily 9.30am–6.30pm | Av. Siam 3 | free shuttle from several hotels every 30 mins | ccsiammall.com*

SPORT & ACTIVITIES

There's a wide range of outdoor activities here, as in the neighbouring town of Los Cristianos.

AQUALAND 👯

A saltwater theme park with pools, water slides and flumes, waterfalls and a lazy river, so you can drift gently through the whole complex. There is also a dolphinarium with daily shows. *Daily 10am–5pm | admission 28 euros, children (3–4 years) 11.50 euros, (5–10) 20 euros | San Eugenio Alto | Autopista del Sur, exit 29 | aqualand. es/tenerife*

BOAT TRIPS & DIVING EXCURSIONS

Puerto Colón's harbour is the centre of the local diving and pleasure boat scene. Two-hour catamaran trips on the *Bonadea* (tel. 922 71 45 00 | bonadea2catamaran.com), with or without food on board, cost from 25 euros. It's 49 euros for an excursion on the double-masted *Shogun* (tel. 227 98 04 49). *Royal Delfin (from 45 euros | tel. 922 75 00 85 | tenerifedolphin. com)* organises daily boat tours to Los Gigantes and Masca. *Safari BOB Diving (55 euros for 20 mins | mobile tel. 670 83 95 16 | bob-diving.com)* offer a unique diving experience where you get to observe the fish on underwater scooters while wearing diving helmets.

INSIDER TIP
Something completely different

GOLF

The 18-hole *Golf Las Américas course (getting there: TF-1, exit 28 | tel. 922 75 20 05 | golflasamericas.com)* is located on 90 hectares of land near the resort. Green fee: 59–102 euros depending on the season, online booking possible.

The 27-hole *Costa Adeje Golf (Finca de los Olivos | getting there: TF-1 to Guía de Isora, exit to La Caleta | tel. 922 71 00 00 | golfcostaadeje.com)* blends perfectly into its environment. Green fee: 98 euros for an 18-hole game. The course has a golf school and a driving range.

A taste of Thailand at the Siam Water Park

SIAM PARK 🏖

Inspired by the architecture of Thailand, Siam Park sees itself as a "Kingdom of Water". Extending over an area of 14 hectares, there are temples, dragons and a market on stilts, as well as eight waterslides – one of which whooshes you through a shark tank. At a sandy artificial beach a wave machine churns out breakers up to 3m high. *Daily 10am–5pm | admission 34 euros, children 23 euros, combined ticket with Loro Parque 58/39.50 euros | Autopista del Sur, exit 28 | free buses from many of the hotels, daily 9.30am–6.30pm, every 30 mins | siampark.net.*

WELLNESS

THALASSO & SPA 🏖

What makes the *Mare Nostrum Spa (tel. 922 75 75 40 | marenostrumspa. es)* in the Mare Nostrum Resort so special is its charming setting and many different physiotherapy, beauty and spa treatments across a huge site.

The *Aqua Club Termal (daily 9am–10pm | C/ Calicia | tel. 922 71 65 55 | aquaclubtermal.com)* in Torviscas Alto has a spa with hydro massage, Roman spa, seawater pool, sauna and much more. It costs 21 euros for 2.5 hours (cheaper rates from 8–10pm). Massage, lymph drainage and other special treatments are extra.

Thai Zen SPAce (daily 9am–9pm | elmiradorgranhotel.com) in the Hotel El Mirador is the most stylish spa in town. Bathe in a minimalist-styled thalasso pool with massaging water jets or an enormous jacuzzi. Other features include treatment showers, hot-and-cold contrast pools and a hammam. As the name suggests there is a Southeast Asian theme to many of the treatments.

INSIDER TIP **Ancient treatments** Physiotherapists give Ayurvedic, Thai and yoga massages using natural oils and essences.

BEACHES

Beneath the promenade at Playa de las Américas and Costa Adeje, many small beaches have been created, all with fine, golden sand and protected from the surf by breakwaters, meaning they are safe for children. From *Playa de Troya* in the south to *Playa La Pinta* beyond Puerto Colón, one beach follows another. The beaches further north are quieter and have more space.

PLAYA DEL CAMISÓN
At the very southern tip of Tenerife, this golden gem of a beach lies at the foot of a palm-lined slope and has a view over Los Cristianos. Near the promenade and the Mare Nostrum Resort, there is no traffic but plenty of cafés and cool beach bars to supply the sun worshippers with food and drink. Walk a bit further along the coastal promenade and you will come

to a very popular spot. At sunset, people flock from miles around to enjoy a cocktail at *Chiringuito Bar (daily | €–€€)* by the Villa Cortés hotel. From here you can look out to the island of La Gomera while you relax with a drink at the end of a long day. **INSIDER TIP** **Sunset with style** The peace will only be broken by surfers trying to catch one final wave.

PLAYA DEL DUQUE
The finest beach is also the furthest north. "Duke's Beach", 600m of pale sand with blue and white changing cabins, is overlooked by some rather grand hotels.

PLAYA DE FAÑABÉ
In a quiet resort of the same name, this 800m beach is ideal for relaxed swimming and sunbathing. The *Seasoul Lounge (daily from 11am | Iberostar Hotel Anthelia | seasoul beachclubs.com)* means you don't need to miss out on the high life. Atop a slight slope at the north end of the beach, they offer cocktails and fresh fish to enjoy with their unbeatable sea view.

NIGHTLIFE

When the neon lights start to flicker on, treat yourself to an aperitif, take a stroll along the promenade or go for a bite to eat. Young people congregate in the *Verónica shopping centre*, the entertainment quarter, or along the main street near *Playa de Troya* – for example at the *Kaluna Beach Club*.

The next generation up (i.e. over 20s), on the other hand, gather in the cool music pub, *Magic (live music daily from 10pm | Av. de las Américas | magicbartenerife.com).*

The Pirámide de Arona, home to the *Hard Rock Café (hardrock.com/cafes/ tenerife)*, has more live events. For information about the latest gay hangouts, consult gaytenerife.net.

CASINO PLAYA DE LAS AMÉRICAS

Games of chance – from blackjack to roulette – are on offer in the basement of the Hotel Gran Tinerfe. *Mon–Thu 8pm–3am, Fri–Sun 8pm–4am | admission free (bring ID) | Av. del Litoral 9 | tel. 922 79 37 12 | casinostenerife.com).*

MAGMA

Pop, classical and folk concerts are organised in this avant-garde building near the motorway. *Av. de los Pueblos | TF-1, exit 28 | tenerifemagma.com*

PIRÁMIDE DE ARONA 🏝

Events staged in the auditorium of this imposing Las Vegas-style pyramid include ballet and flamenco evenings with the famous choreographer Carmen Mota, also available with dinner. *Programme in the information kiosk on Av. de las Américas | tel. 922 75 75 49 | marenostrumresort.com*

Shimmering blue sea, fine sand, pine trees and parasols: Playa del Duque

AROUND PLAYA DE LAS AMÉRICAS/ COSTA ADEJE

3 LA CALETA

4 km/50 mins north of Las Américas (walking along the promenade)

Once a quiet fishing village with a view over the developing coast, La Caleta itself has long since been swallowed up by tourism. Its posh hotels and golf course provide plenty of evidence, as does the promenade which you can use to walk to Los Cristianos.

La Caleta's fish restaurants have largely survived, even if rustic dives have been transformed into large, comfortable restaurants. Right by the water's edge is *La Caleta* restaurant *(daily | tel. 922 78 06 75 | €€)*. The open terrace above the cliffs has great views. The long menu includes a wide selection of tapas, and fish (of varying quality). Next door, the terrace restaurant *La Masía del Mar & Piscis (daily | C/ del Muelle 3 | tel. 922 71 08 95 | masiadelmar.com | €€)* has a better reputation: the delicious fish soup is served in small copper pots, and you can pick your fish from their tanks. *D10*

INSIDER TIP
The freshest fish around

4 ADEJE

7km/10 mins north of Las Américas on the TF-1

Most visitors just pass through this sleepy place on their way to "Hell's Gorge" *(Barranco del Infierno)*. However, it is a very interesting place in itself. At the beginning of the 16th century, Spanish conquerors built the church of *Santa Úrsula (C/ Grande)*, with its beautifully carved wooden ceiling. The stunning baroque altar came later. The square outside is perhaps even more beautiful, serving as a kind of gateway to the gorge. It's a perfect spot to get a first glimpse of the huge Barranco del Infierno.

Local farmers come to sell their produce at the pleasant and relaxed ☂ *Agromercado (Sat, Sun 8am–2pm | C/ Archajara)*, where you can buy fruit, vegetables, goat's cheese, aniseed bread and much more. At the upper end of *Calle de los Molinos*, *Restaurante Otelo (closed Tue | tel. 922 78 03 74 | FB: Restauranteotelo | €–€€)* boasts great views over Adeje. This is also the start of a beautiful walk into the ⭐ *Barranco del Infierno (daily 8am–2.30pm (gorge open until 6pm), total hiking time approx. 3hrs, 6.5km | admission 15 euros | access only with prior reservation online or at the information stand at the entrance to the gorge | barrancodelinfierno.es)*. Helmets are mandatory (can be hired) due to the danger of falling rocks. A former shepherd's path winds its way up into the exposed, barren mountains. Later as you approach the narrow, shaded "Hell's Gorge" with its meandering stream, the vegetation

Colourful woodcarving: altarpiece and ceiling in Adeja's Iglesia Santa Ursula

becomes less sparse. And when you reach the end of the gorge, you will find a waterfall that drops over 80m. *E10*

5 ARONA

8km/10 mins north of Las Américas on the TF-28/TF-51

Overshadowed by the huge Roque del Conde, it is hard to believe that this sleepy town is the administrative centre responsible for the two seemingly inexhaustible gold mines of Los Cristianos and Playa de las Américas. Very few of the many billions of euros spent in the Arona area ends up here but it does boast an attractive town hall beside a square shaded by laurels and a church dating from 1627. *E-F10*

6 ÁGUILAS JUNGLE PARK

9km/10 mins northeast of Las Américas on the TF-1/TF-28

A jungle on Tenerife? Up above the resorts, 7 hectares of land have been turned into a patch of rainforest that includes lakes and waterfalls. You can watch eagles, vultures, falcons, owls and other raptors hunting (and being fed by their handler). You can also marvel at white tigers, lions, penguins, hippos, crocodiles and orangutans. The park is rounded off with a cactus garden, climbing frames and … pedalos. *Daily 10am–5.30pm | admission 27 euros, children aged 3–4 10.50, 5–10 19 euros| getting there: Ctra Los Cristianos–Arona Km3 (TF-1, junction 27) | free buses from the resorts in the south | www.aguilasjunglepark.com | 3–4hrs E11*

🛇 PLAYA PARAÍSO

11km/15 mins northwest of Las Américas (on the TF-1/TF-47)

The name "Paradise Beach" is a slight exaggeration. But there are two small sand bays which are great for swimming. The resort's eye-catcher is a twin tower: the *Hard Rock Hotel (624 rooms | Av. de Adeje | tel. 971 92 76 91 | hardrockhotels.com/tenerife | €€€)*. Its rooftop bar, *The 16th*, is chic and stylish. Up here on the large terrace you can enjoy the view along with live music (from blues to funk) most evenings. *📖 D10*

INSIDER TIP
A cool place to cool down

LOS GIGANTES

(📖 C8) **This was once the small fishing village of Puerto de Santiago But the tourism boom added two new developments to it: Playa de la Arena is named after its beach, and ⭐ Los Gigantes, to the north, after the "gigantic" cliffs that rise 450m from the waves. The marvellous landscape stands in contrast with row upon row of giant, ugly, identical-looking hotels.**

The coastal road comes to an end at *Los Gigantes*. The resort shares a name

It's always a treat to see dolphins from a boat

THE SOUTHWEST

with the cliffs, which is fitting as its steep streets cling on to them for dear life. The place to be here is *Poblado Marinero* marina, where yachts bob around in front of the dramatic backdrop.

EATING & DRINKING

DELI ON THE HILL

Fresh salads, snacks, sandwiches and home-made cake served in pretty surroundings: a good spot to chill out. *Closed Sun | Ctra General Puerto Santiago 32 | tel. 628 50 01 63 | delionthehill.eu | €*

EL RINCÓN DE JUAN CARLOS

A Michelin star … here? Hidden in a courtyard behind the church at Los Gigantes lurks El Rincón where the Padrón family make creative Canarian dishes that look and taste incredible.

INSIDER TIP
A gastronomic gem

They do this in a relaxed, stress-free atmosphere, which happily rubs off on the customers. *Only evenings, closed Sun | Pasaje Jacaranda 2 | tel. 922 86 80 40 | elrincondejuancarlos.com | €€€ (menus start at 55 euros)*

RESTAURANTE PANCHO

This beach restaurant at Playa de la Arena offers fine cuisine and has won several awards. The smoked fish is

INSIDER TIP
Haute cuisine at the beach

tasty, as is the duck breast in honey sauce. And if you want to treat yourself, order the excellent six-course menu of the season for just 40 euros. *Closed Mon | Av. Marítima 26 | tel. 922 86 13 23 | restaurantepancho.es | €€*

SPORT & ACTIVITIES

BOAT TRIPS

The best way to see Los Gigantes is from the water. The former shrimper *Katrin* is just one of a number of boats that bring sightseers to the cliffs *(daily from 11.30am | 2-hr trip 25 euros | 100m from the harbour entrance on the right | tel. 922 86 03 32)*. They also offer dolphin watching. The catamaran *Nashiro Uno* also organises one- to three-hour whale- and dolphin-watching tours from the *harbour (daily 10.45am, 1.45pm and 4pm | 20–40 euros, depending on duration | maritimaacantilados.com)*.

BEACHES

PLAYA DE LA ARENA ★ 🏖

A truly beautiful place with 300m of jet-black volcanic sand contrasting with the bright green palm trees. The beach is the island's sunniest spot and has regularly been awarded the European Blue Flag for the cleanliness of its water and sand. It also has excellent facilities with sun loungers (to hire), toilets and lifeguards.

PLAYA DE LOS GUÍOS

The big beach at Playa de los Guíos starts at the Poblado Marinero marina. A great location under the cliffs is also a reason for caution due to falling rocks; make sure you pick a spot nearer the water!

The views are amazing along the TF 38 between Teide National Park and Chio

AROUND LOS GIGANTES

⑧ PLAYA DE ALCALÁ

6km/10 mins south of Los Gigantes on theTF-47

The luxurious *Palacio de Isora* hotel in Alcalá is the sort of place that other hotels look up to. This vast complex in southern Spanish style is situated by a rocky beach with views of La Gomera. The fishing village around it with its simple houses and pretty harbour seems to belong to a completely different (and bygone) world. *▥ C8*

⑨ SAN JUAN

8.5km/12 mins south of Los Gigantes on theTF-47

The luxury *Ritz Carlton Abama* resort emerges from San Juan like a rusty mirage and looks like a Moroccan fort. It even has its own golf course. There are villa complexes on several levels running right down to the sea. With a park, seven pools, a spa and a funicular down to the bright beach below, it's simply the best.

From the road San Juan appears somewhat dull but if you head to the harbour, you'll see it has retained some of its former charm with an attractive artificial sandy beach, promenade and lots of restaurants. *▥ C9*

Delicias del Sol (Mon–Fri 10am–3pm, Sat 10am–2pm | main road TF-82 at Km32.5 | deliciasdelsol.eu), run by Gerrit and Amanda, everything has been grown organically on the island . From local wines to jams and chutneys made using exotic fruit, and *mojo* sauces and sambals in a

> **INSIDER TIP**
> Mouth-wateringly good

range of flavours, you will find everything you could ever want here.

The TF-38 begins just north of Chío and is one of three roads leading to Teide National Park. It is a wonderful drive, beginning alongside fields then heading up to the barren volcanoes above 2,000m. The TF-375 will take you to the ceramics museum in Arguayo (see p. 30). To reach Santiago del Teide, take the TF-82 via Tamaimo or the motorway which runs alongside it.

🔟 GUÍA DE ISORA

16km/26 mins southeast of Los Gigantes on the TF-454 and TF-82

Many resort employees live in cheap, makeshift buildings in this village. If you want to see the more attractive side of Guía de Isora (pop. 5,200) head to the historical centre above the main road. The handsome *Iglesia Nuestra Señora de la Luz* on the church square is a reminder that much wealth was created here in the 16th century. 🗺 D8

🔟 CHÍO

12km/20 mins east of Los Gigantes on the TF-454 and TF-82

If you love great food shops, make sure to visit Chío. In the wonderful

WHERE TO STAY

MAR Y SOL

Queen Letizia of Spain presented this hotel with an award for being among the best hotels in Europe for people with disabilities. *The Spa & Sport Mar y Sol (Av. Amsterdam 8 | tel. 922 75 05 40 | marysol.org | €€)* in Los Cristianos is completely wheelchair accessible from its jacuzzi to its gym, diving school and golf course. The owner, Mr Fischer, proudly says "this is a very special all-inclusive hotel. We want to include everyone whether they have a disability or not. That is our goal".

DISCOVERY TOURS

Want to get under the skin of the region? Then our discovery tours are the ideal guide – they provide advice on which sights to visit, tips on where to stop for that perfect holiday snap, a choice of the best places to eat and drink, and suggestions for fun activities.

❶ TENERIFE IN TWO DAYS

➤ Spain's highest mountain
➤ Stunning "lunar landscape" and crystal-clear air
➤ Strings of beaches in different shades

📍	Puerto de la Cruz		Puerto de la Cruz
↻	260km	🚗	2 days (7 hrs total driving time)

ⓘ Driving on the mountain roads takes time
Note: if it snows, the road to the national park may be closed

Mount Teide bugloss blooms despite the arid conditions

ATTRACTIVE & ATMOSPHERIC

It is worth setting off early because the busiest time in the national park and on the Teide cable car is around midday. Start in ❶ Puerto de la Cruz ➤ p. 42 and *head south* through the densely populated Valle de la Orotava ➤ p. 50, first to the picturesque village of ❷ La Orotava ➤ p. 50 where romantic plazas, churches and monasteries serve as reminders of the island's colonial past. *Carry on along the TF-21. Above Aguamansa* is La Caldera ➤ p. 54, the green crater which is now a picnic area and starting point for hiking tours into the pine forest. Between Km22 and 23, stop to take a look at La Margarita de Piedra, a large naturally formed basalt rosette, remnant of the era when there was much volcanic activity here.

PEAK TENERIFE IN THE NATIONAL PARK

At an altitude of 2,000m the forest thins and volcanic rock takes over. With an attractive visitor centre, ❸ El Portillo ➤ p. 64 acts as the "gateway" to the Las Cañadas crater and the National Park ➤ p. 61. A rock garden contains all the plants that have adapted to the extreme alpine climate; the finest is the Mount Teide bugloss, a sparking red perennial that grows to a height

DAY 1

❶ Puerto de la Cruz

7km   10mins

❷ La Orotava

26.5 km   27mins

❸ El Portillo

13km   15mins

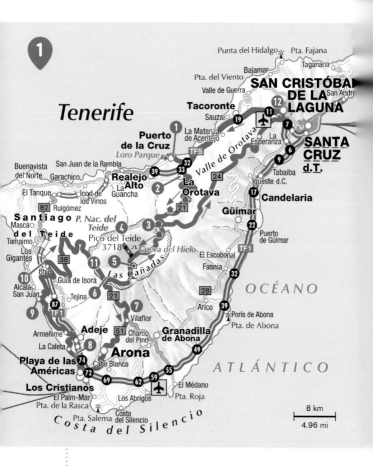

Tenerife

of about 2m. As you continue your journey, the road crosses lava and ash fields in white, green, red, grey and pitch black. They bear witness to the volcanic activity, which formed the island millions of years ago. *At Km43, you'll reach the turn-off to the station for the cable car,* which, in just a few minutes, takes you from 2,300m to the ❹ **summit station** at 3,555m, almost at the top of **Mount Teide** ➤ p. 63. The view from the top (3,718m) is amazing.

❹ summit station

8.5 km   5mins

FOLLOW THE CRATER

The next stop is at the Roques de García ➤ p. 63, giant, weathered rock formations that sit majestically above a plateau surrounded by jagged rocks. Take a break at nearby ❺ Parador Nacional ➤ p. 65. Both its cafeteria and rustic restaurant *(€-€€)* have impressive views of Mount Teide. There are also great views from the 5m-high Zapato de la Reina, or "Queen's Shoe", and the ❻ Boca de Tauce, a gap in the crater rim. *You now leave Las Cañadas crater and follow the TF-21 down through the sparse pine forest to* ❼ Vilaflor ➤ p. 96, a mountain village at an altitude of almost 1,500m. Enjoy a hearty meal at Rincón del Roberto before spending the night at Spa Villalba *(27 rooms | Ctra San Roque 4 | tel. 922 70 99 30 | hotelvillalba.com | €€).*

BUSY BEACHES, PEACEFUL FORESTS

While Vilaflor is often hidden in the clouds, the village of Arona ➤ p. 115, *just 12km away*, gets bathed in light from the south. You are now leaving the peace of the mountains and heading for the heart of Tenerife's tourism industry. Drive down to the coast where a 12km promenade links the resorts, from Los Cristianos to La Caleta, with beaches every few hundred metres. The best of them, ❽ Bahía del Duque ➤ p. 107 , is surrounded by spectacular hotels. There are some excellent fish restaurants in La Caleta ➤ p. 114, but hold off until you reach ❾ San Juan ➤ p. 118 , a quiet fishing village with a row of harbour restaurants.

ROAD TRIP WITH A VIEW

After your meal, *take the TF-463 up to* Chío, where you can purchase some of the island's delicacies – including almond mousse and organic wine – at ❿ Delicias del Sol ➤ p. 119 *(TF-82 at Km32.5).* Then, *on the TF-38,* you'll plunge into a beautiful volcanic landscape dotted with pine trees. From the ⓫ Mirador Chío you can look out across swathes of black volcanic debris to the Pico Viejo ➤ p. 62, Mount Teide's younger brother. At the Boca de Tauce you'll *re-join the TF-21 mountain road,* which is so spectacular that you won't mind returning along it in the opposite direction. *On the way back turn*

❺ Parador Nacional

7km   7mins

❻ Boca de Tauce

15.5 km   15mins

❼ Vilaflor

25km   25mins

DAY 2

❽ Bahía del Duque

19.5 km   20mins

❾ San Juan

14km   13mins

❿ Delicias del Sol

25 km   25 mins

⓫ Mirador Chío

onto the TF-24 – the "island's backbone" – at El Portillo. After a few kilometres, you'll pass the entrance to the futuristic Observatorio del Teide ➤ p. 64, and *at Km32* you will pass through the black, white and yellow rock formations known as La Tarta ("The Tart"). After that it's back into the pine forest. There are plenty of clearings with viewpoints offering vistas out to the east, northwest and occasionally over to the islands of La Palma and Gran Canaria.

APERITIF ON THE BEACH

After so much nature, it's now time for a spot of culture: ⑫ La Laguna ➤ p. 76, a UNESCO World Heritage Site, is a picturesque town whose cobbled, pedestrianised streets are lined with churches, monasteries and palaces. A hearty meal can be enjoyed at La Bourmet ➤ p. 79. From La Laguna, *take the TF-5 motorway* back to ① Puerto de la Cruz for an early evening swim. The pitch-black Playa Jardín ➤ p. 48 ("Garden Beach") is the perfect place for a sunset dip. Then relax over a cocktail in one of the shady beach bars.

71.5km 1h 10mins

⑫ La Laguna

29.5km 22mins

① Puerto de la Cruz

La Laguna is pristine and picturesque

❷ ANAGA: LAUREL FOREST & A PRETTY BEACH

➤ Learn about laurel
➤ A series of switchbacks to the wild coast
➤ Round it off at the white Teresitas beach

📍 La Laguna

🏁 Santa Cruz de Tenerife

→ 86km

🚗 1 day
(2 hrs total driving time)

ℹ️ From the north: From Puerto de la Cruz/La Orotava take the TF-5 (30 mins) to ❶ La Laguna.
From the south: take the TF-1 (1.5 hrs) to ❶ La Laguna.

ENJOY THE VIEWS

Start in ❶ La Laguna ➤ p. 76 and *take the beautiful TF-12 to* Las Mercedes where the laurel forest begins. *At Km25.1,* make a stop at the ❷ Mirador de Jardina, from where you can survey Mount Teide and over half the island. Soon after, *at Km22.7,* you will reach the ❸ Mirador Cruz del Carmen where a well-camouflaged visitor centre ➤ p. 85, will give you information about all the footpaths in the region. Even an hour's easy walking will give you a good sense of the laurel forest. Cruz del Carmen also has a tiny chapel and the rustic bistro La Gangochera ➤ p. 85, where almost everything is locally sourced. Try the cress soup.

INSIDER TIP
Super soup

SWITCHBACKS

Continue along the road. The next viewpoint, at Km21.8, the ❹ Mirador Pico del Inglés, provides a different panorama over the northwest and northeast coasts. *If you turn off the TF-12 you can explore remote hamlets,* such as Las Carboneras, Chinamada or Taborno. ❺ Casas de Afur *is especially quaint (fork left at Km18.4).* Back on the TF-12, continue along the high

❶ La Laguna	
8 km	10 mins
❷ Mirador de Jardina	
2.5km	2mins
❸ Mirador Cruz del Carmen	
4km	4mins
❹ Mirador Pico del Inglés	
11km	11mins
❺ Casas de Afur	
20km	19mins

mountain road and at Km11.4 you'll reach a confusing junction. A left turn would take you on the TF-123 to El Bailadero, where sheep and goats were once herded. However, you need to start your descent on the TF-12 (towards San Andrés). After 1km, take a left and go through a tunnel before joining the TF-134 towards Taganana/Benijo. A series of switchbacks along sharply defined ridges provides magnificent views of the landscape and the cliffs below. There are not many places to stop and take photos until you reach ❻ Taganana.

❻ Taganana

9.5km 19mins

BACK TO THE COAST

After this dizzying stretch, you've earned some seafood. On this rocky coastline restaurants offering great views of the wild sea can be found in Roque de las Bodegas – i.e. the authentic Canarian ❼ Casa África (daily | Roque de las Bodegas 3 | tel. 922 59 01 00 | €–€€), where the friendly Señora África cooks up traditional specialities – and in ❽ Benijo with its pretty beach.

❼ Casa África

2km 2mins

❽ Benijo

LAST STOP: TOP BEACH

After visiting Benijo turn round and *head back uphill and, from the spine of the Anaga Mountains, follow the switchbacks down the TF-12 to the eastern side of island* and the fishing and seaside resort of ❾ San Andrés ➤ p. 76. If you're hungry, grab a bite to eat here and enjoy a swim at Tenerife's finest beach, the Playa de las Teresitas. *Now head along the coast to the capital* ❿ Santa Cruz de Tenerife ➤ p. 70. From there either head back to the north via La Laguna or take the TF-1 motorway back to your resort.

18km	18mins

❾ San Andrés

12km	21mins

❿ Santa Cruz de Tenerife

The original beach at Benijo in the northeast is only suitable for swimming at low tide

➌ TENO: GORGES & GORGEOUS VILLAGES

➤ Rugged mountains and a stunning village
➤ The lighthouse at the end of the island
➤ The island's thousand-year-old resident

📍 Los Gigantes

🏁 Los Gigantes
1 day

🔄 110km

🚗 (2 hrs total driving time)

Kit list: warm jacket, sturdy shoes
Note: The TF-445 towards ➎ **Punta de Teno** is closed after it has rained and in high winds due to the risk of falling rocks; there is a shuttle bus at weekends. Masca gorge is also closed after rain.

➊ Los Gigantes

14.5km   17mins

➋ Arguayo

11km   10mins

WINDING MOUNTAIN ROADS

➊ Los Gigantes ➤ p. 116 are striking rocky cliffs which rise to 450m above the village of the same name, dwarfing its houses, boats and people. These "Giants", located at the southern end of the Teno Massif, give a foretaste of the inaccessible mountains where you will spend your day. *The TF-454 first climbs through hairpin bends on its way up to Santiago del Teide,* passing banana and tomato plantations. *At Km11, make a detour to* ➋ Arguayo ➤ p. 61, a traditional village known for its ceramics. Visitors are welcome to watch the skilled potters at work and purchase their products in an old, restored workshop.

WILD NATURE

After Santiago del Teide ➤ p. 61, the landscape becomes more dramatic: everywhere you look are steep cliffs, rugged rocks and hardy plants. Erosion has gnawed away at the volcanic rock of the Teno Mountains ➤ p.59, a very ancient geological formation. From the Mirador de Cherfe you get your first glimpse of ❸ Masca ➤ p. 60, a hamlet tucked between sheer rock walls, which was not joined up to the road network until the 1980s. It is divided between several rocky outcrops and a tour through this dispersed village will involve treading carefully on crooked cobblestones.

It has several small restaurants. *For a few kilometres, the narrow road winds its way through the mountains.* The Mirador de Hilda has a café and terrace and splendid views back up the Masca valley. From the Mirador de Baracán, on the next pass, you'll have a view of the gentler hills in the north.

INSIDER TIP
Have a look behind you

ALONG THE STEEP CLIFFS
Drive through the village of Las Portelas and head down to Buenavista del Norte ➤ p. 59 where you can enjoy excellent seafood on the coast at ❹ El Burgado *(daily | Playa de la Arena | tel. 902 09 17 55 | €€). From Buenavista, the remote TF-445 runs along Tenerife's*

❸ Masca

19km 21mins

❹ El Burgado

10km 10mins

Masca is a beautiful hamlet in a magnificent mountainous landscape

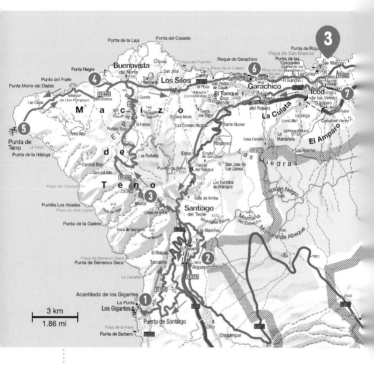

rocky northwestern coastline. Drive carefully in bad weather! Falling rocks are not uncommon after heavy rain. The journey comes to an end at ❺ Punta de Teno ➤ p. 60, where you can jump into the waves in a sheltered bay at the foot of the high cliffs.

❺ Punta de Teno

18.5km   18mins

THOUSAND-YEAR-OLD TREE?

After so much wilderness, a bit of town-life might be in order. *Return to Buenavista and continue on the TF-42 until you reach* ❻ Garachico ➤ p. 56, where the Old Town – with fort, monastery and colonial houses – is a splendid example of Tenerife's traditional architecture. The volcanic coast is also worth a look – you can enjoy the view over a meal on the terrace of El Caletón *(daily | Av. Tomé Cano | tel. 922 13 3301 | €€).* After your break, *continue on the TF-42 to* ❼ Icod de los Vinos ➤ p. 54, where you will find the Drago Milenario, a dragon tree believed to be 1,000 years old and one of Tenerife's

❻ Garachico

5.5km   5mins

❼ Icod de los Vinos

most recognised landmarks. The streets here are pretty and lined with grand houses. Have a free glass of wine in one of the food shops. *Now head back in the direction of Puerto de Santiago* along a less dramatic but equally beautiful mountain road *through El Tanque, Erjos and Santiago del Teide to your starting point at* ❶ Los Gigantes.

❹ WALKING AMONG THE ROQUES DE GARCÍA

➤ The top of the island
➤ *Clash of the Titans* film location
➤ A mysterious "cathedral"

◉	Mirador de la Ruleta	🏁	Mirador de la Ruleta
↻	4.5km	🚶	Total walking time 1¾ hrs
▮▮▮	Difficulty: medium	↗	Ascent: 110m

ℹ️ Bus: From Puerto de la Cruz take bus no. 348 at 9.30am to its final stop at Parador; from Costa Adeje/Las Américas take bus no. 342. Return around 4pm.
Car: If you're driving, take the TF-21 to Km46.4. Park at the Mirador de la Ruleta. There's also a car park at Parador. Don't leave anything in your car!

VIEW OVER THE PLATEAU
From your starting point at the ❶ Mirador de la Ruleta, take a few steps in the *direction of the TF-21 and turn left immediately behind the group of rocks along a wide path signposted "Sendero 3".* The path ascends gradually past the foot of the ❷ Roques de García ➤ p. 63, which have been formed by wind and rain over the course of millions of years. The path soon narrows and follows the edge of an old lava field. *Thirty minutes after*

❶ Mirador de la Ruleta

300m 4mins

❷ Roques de García

1300m 20mins

3 Torre Blanca	
1300m 23mins	

setting off, you'll pass the **3 Torre Blanca** (White Tower), the last in the series of gigantic rock formations. A natural plateau has been carved out here offering a vast panoramic view over the Ucanca plain. *Shortly after the plateau, the path veers left down to the plain,* with the craggy foot of the Roques de García rising up in front of you. When the path becomes unclear, cairns have been used to mark the route.

NATURE'S ARCHITECTURE

4 "Cathedral"	
600m 23mins	

You'll quickly spot your next destination, **4 "Cathedral"**, a 100-m-high solitary rock rising up from the plateau – its vertical faces are popular with rock climbers. *Before reaching the "Cathedral", the route bends left and climbs steeply up a sharply bending path.* This, the most strenuous section of the walk, brings you up to the viewpoint

5 Mirador de la Ruleta	
500m 7mins	

at the **5 Mirador de la Ruleta**. Take in the vast, desolate Ucanca plain from which the giant rocks rise like prehistoric stones with the rugged walls of Las Cañadas in the background.

TIME FOR SOME REFRESHMENT

Walk along the access road to the mirador until you reach the TF-21. Cross the road and go directly to the pale purple building of the ❻ Parador Nacional ➤ p. 65. Continue 450m further on until you reach the cafeteria for a snack or the rustic restaurant for Canarian specialities while taking one long last look at Mount Teide before heading back to your starting point at the ❶ Mirador de la Ruleta.

INSIDER TIP
break with a view

❻ **Parador Nacional**	
500m	6mins
❶ **Mirador de la Ruleta**	

❺ CYCLING AROUND THE SOUTHERN HILLS

➤ Explore the hills behind the southern beach resorts
➤ Viewpoints, volcanic rocks and historic towns
➤ Tenerife's longest beach

📍	Los Cristianos	🏁	Los Cristianos
🔄	63km	🚲	1 day (6 hrs total cycling time)
📶	Difficulty: medium		

ℹ️ Cost: Mountain bike rental from 16 euros; admission **Jungle Park** and sculpture park **Mariposa** 26 euros each; admission ❿ **Reserva Ambiental** incl. tour 15 euros. Note: You have to wear a helmet in Spain

ARONA & A SCULPTURE PARK

Leave ❶ Los Cristianos ➤ p. 102 *on the TF-665 (signposted Chayofa/Arona). After the motorway roundabout, take the TF-28* and leave the town behind you. The traffic ebbs away and the scenery becomes more rural. As you start to go uphill, you can look back at the resorts on the coast from a safe distance. Stop for a first coffee break in

❶ **Los Cristianos**	
4km	31mins

② Chayofa	
6.5km 1h 8mins	
③ Arona	
1km 3mins	
④ Túnez	
5.5km 31mins	
⑤ Mirador de la Centinela	
4.5km 23mins	
⑥ San Miguel	
5.5km 37mins	
⑦ Granadilla de Abona	
12.5km 42mins	
⑧ El Médano	
7km 26mins	

② Chayofa, where foreign residents live in flower-adorned bungalows. A former tomato plantation, Mesón Chayofa *(daily | C/ El Taroso 43 | tel. 922 72 91 89 | €€)* offers food and drinks in peaceful surroundings; another attraction is the Jungle Park *(daily 10am–5.30pm | www.aguilasjunglepark.com)* which has tigers, sea lions, monkeys and a falconry show. From here, *continue along a road which joins the TF-51* which will take you up to the town of **③** Arona ➤ p. 115 at an altitude of 630m with high mountains around it. It has an attractive plaza with a town hall, church and dense laurel trees in whose shade you can take a quick snooze. You then *head towards* **④** Túnez *along a side road* where two gallery owners have created Mariposa *(C/ Túnez 63-A | kulturpark-mariposa.com)*, a two-hectare art and sculpture park.

AMAZING VIEWS & OLD-FASHIONED VILLAGES

In Valle de San Lorenzo, you return to the TF-28 and, after a few kilometres, you reach the **⑤** Mirador de la Centinela, which has the best views in the south; you can enjoy them from restaurant La Centinela *(closed Mon | FB: miradorlacentinela | €–€€)*. The road now begins to roll gently (but no steep hills!) to **⑥** San Miguel, with its pretty church, cobbled streets and the ethnographic museum Casa del Capitán *(closed Sat/Sun | C/ Calvario 1)*. It's another 4km to **⑦** Granadilla de Abona, a village which has grown hugely thanks to the tourism boom. However, its historic centre has retained its old charm. Next to the parish church and worth a visit is the former post office. Today it is the Hotel Rural Senderos de Abona *(C/ Peatonal de la Iglesia 5 | www.senderosdeabona.es | €)*. As well as the restaurant's terrace, the hotel features a curiosity cabinet stuffed full of weird and wonderful objects.

THE BLISS OF THE DOWNHILL

Beyond Granadilla, you come to a well-earned downhill stretch: *zoom down the TF-64, continue 7.5km to the coast and over the TF-1 motorway until you reach* **⑧** El Médano ➤ p. 93, 5km away. This, Tenerife's surfer paradise, has the longest natural beach on the island: it

SIDER TIP
Pick your beach carefully

stretches for 3km at the foot of the Montaña Roja (Red Mountain). Take a dip in the waves! Playa de la Tejita ➤ p. 94, the beach just west of the Montaña Roja, is a popular nudist spot.

FRESH FISH AT THE HARBOUR

Now take the TF-643 along the coast to your next treat: the rows of restaurants and bars offering fresh seafood at the harbour in Los Abrigos ➤ p. 95 – ❾ Perlas del Mar ➤ p. 95, for example. After your meal, it's time to visit the ❿ Reserva Ambiental. In the gorge behind the five-star resort of *San Blas (Av. Greñamora 1)* to the west of Los Abrigos, you can immerse yourself in the magical volcanic landscape – and even indulge in a boat trip. An interactive museum offers an insight into Tenerife's nature and history. *Head back to* ❶ Los Cristianos *on the flat TF-655;* it's an easy ride home!

❾ **Perlas del Mar**

2km 10mins

❿ **Reserva Ambiental**

14km 1h 6mins

❶ **Los Cristianos**

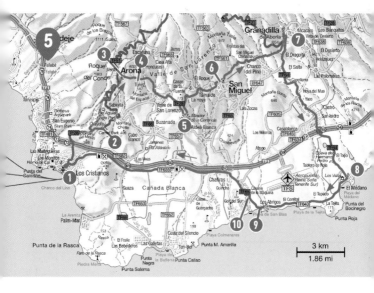

GOOD TO KNOW

HOLIDAY BASICS

ARRIVAL

AIR

Cheap flights are available from the UK and Ireland with Ryanair, easyJet and Thomas Cook (UK flight time about four hours). Book ahead and look out for deals to get the best prices – a return fare can cost anything between £30 and £350. There are two airports: the southern airport, *Reina Sofía* (aka *Tenerife Sur*), which is served by most international airlines,

is a 20-minute drive from Playa de las Américas and Los Cristianos and about one hour from Puerto de la Cruz. Scheduled buses run from the southern airport to Los Cristianos and Costa Adeje (nos. 40, 343 and 711; approx. 3.50 euros), Santa Cruz de Tenerife (nos. 111 and 711; approx. 9 euros) and Puerto de la Cruz (no. 343; approx. 10 euros).

All Spanish internal flights and many low-cost airlines land at *Tenerife Norte* near La Laguna. Inter-Canary Island flights depart from here and also from *Reina Sofía* (information tel. 922 39 20 37).

FERRY

Once a week at 5pm a car ferry operated by *Compañía Trasmediterránea-Acciona* leaves from the southern Spanish port of Cádiz. The crossing to Santa Cruz de Tenerife takes 31 hours. A fare for a single journey starts from 200 euros

 No time difference

The Canary Islands operate on Western European Time (the same as GMT) from November to March and on Western European Summer Time (GMT +1) from April to October.

Teide National Park

per person (in a four-bed cabin). A car costs roughly the same. Book through travel agencies or *trasmediterranea.es*.

Adapter Type C

220 Volt alternating current. You will need a European adapter.

GETTING IN

All arrivals from the UK will be required to show a passport on arrival which must have at least six months' validity and must have been issued during the 10 years immediately before the date of entry. Check any other requirements with your airline before you fly.

WHEN TO GO

Tenerife's mild climate means only small fluctuations in temperature. In the arid south, even in winter, temperatures hardly ever fall below 18°C and only rarely rise above 24°C. In summer the temperature can stay at 30°C and above for weeks. Even at moderate altitudes weak air currents can give rise to oppressive heat. The temperatures in the north are often significantly lower than in the south. In winter it can get cold at altitudes above 500m. A good rule of thumb is that it drops 1°C per 100m of altitude. However, even if it is very hot on the coast, it may be freezing in the Teide region. So, remember to pack a rain jacket and sweater along with your sun cream.

As water temperatures in Tenerife are always in the 18–24°C range, it's fine to swim in the sea 365 days a year. The best time to visit the island is from November to March.

GETTING AROUND

BUS

Buses on Tenerife are called *guaguas* (pro- nounced guahuah). Green TITSA buses run from Santa Cruz's central bus station, *Estación de Guaguas (Av. 3 de Mayo 47)* to almost every town on Tenerife. You can buy a multi-fare, "Ten +" ticket at bus stations in Santa Cruz and other holiday resorts. This gives holders a 30 per cent (or more) reduction on all fares (it does not apply on the nos 342/348 which go to Teide). Information is available in Spanish and English Mon–Fri 7am–9pm on *922 53 13 00* and also on the internet at titsa.com. Tram no. 1 runs every 5–15 minutes between Santa Cruz and the university town of La Laguna *(metrotenerife.com)*.

CAR HIRE

Car rental companies run offices in the airports, in all the holiday resorts and also in many hotels. Hire charges for a small car could well be less than 25 euros per day (including taxes and comprehensive insurance). *Cicar (tel. 928 82 29 00 | cicar.com)* is a reliable local company, which has offices in every port and airport and most holiday resorts. The cars are well maintained, and the service is excellent if you break down. You must be over 21 to rent a car and firms will require a deposit.

RULES OF THE ROAD

The roads on Tenerife are good and safe. Maximum speed: in built up areas 50 km/h; on country roads 90 km/h; and on motorways 120 km/h. The breath-alcohol limit is 0.025%, which roughly corresponds to a blood-alcohol limit of 0.05% (stricter

FESTIVALS & EVENTS
ALL YEAR ROUND

JANUARY/FEBRUARY
Festival de Música de Canarias (Santa Cruz de Tenerife): Internationally renowned classical music festival, *festivaldecanarias.com*

FEBRUARY/MARCH
⭐ *Carnaval*: week-long fiesta, begins in Santa Cruz then spreads across the island, *carnavaltenerife.com*

MARCH/APRIL
Semana Santa (La Laguna): Magnificent processions climaxing with the silent march on Good Friday

MAY
Fiesta de San Isidro (Granadilla/Los Realejos/La Orotava): Celebrations (photo) take place around 15 May in honour of the patron saint of farmers

MAY/JUNE
Corpus Christi (La Orotava): Stunning flowery "carpets" of volcanic sand are laid in streets and squares (see p. 54)

JULY
Nuestra Señora del Carmen (Santa Cruz de Tenerife/Puerto de la Cruz): Beautiful boat procession on 16 July

AUGUST
Romería de la Virgen de Candelaria (Candelaria): On 15 August tens of thousands of pilgrims make their way to Candelaria to pay homage to the island's patron saint
Romería de San Roque (Garachico): On 16 August the patron's party and parades move to Garachico

SEPTEMBER
Festival Sabandeño, *Fiestas del Cristo* (La Laguna): Canarian folk bands play to huge crowds

NOVEMBER
Festival Foto-Noviembre (Santa Cruz/La Laguna): A biennial photography festival which encourages photographers to exhibit raw and provocative work, *fotonoviembre.com*

than the UK). Drivers must also keep a yellow vest in the car. Telephone calls may only be made using hands-free mobile phones.

Parking is not allowed where there are yellow markings by the kerb; a parking fee is payable where there are blue lines. Only licensed *grúas* are permitted to tow away vehicles.

TAXI

All taxis are licensed and fitted with meters which must be turned on when you get into the car. On top of the basic fare, you pay supplements on Sundays and national holidays, at night and for port/airport trips as well as for bulky luggage. If you want to take a taxi for a day's tour, get a quote first.

TRAVELLING BETWEEN THE ISLANDS

You can get to all the other Canary Islands from Tenerife. Ferries companies such as Fred Olsen *(fredolsen.es)* and Naviera Armas *(navieraarmas. com)* generally charge about the same as flights using the regional carriers,

RESPONSIBLE TRAVEL

Being environmentally friendly whilst travelling is not just about your carbon footprint en route to and from your holiday destination. It's also about protecting nature and culture abroad. If you would like to find out more about eco-tourism please visit: www. ecotourism.org.

Binter *(binternet.com)* and Canary Fly *(canaryfly.es)*.

EMERGENCIES

EMBASSIES & CONSULATES
UK CONSULATE
Mon–Fri 8.30am–1.30pm | Plaza Weyler, 8, 1° | 38003 Santa Cruz de Tenerife | tel. 928 26 25 08

US CONSULATE
Edificio ARCA | C/ Los Martínez Escobar, 3, Oficina 7 | 35007 Las Palmas | tel. 928 27 12 59

EMERGENCY SERVICES
Dial 112 in an emergency for access to ambulance, fire, police and emergency medical service.

HEALTH
A good travel insurance policy will enable you to access local medical services. If you have to pay up front, ask for a detailed bill *(factura)* in order to get reimbursed later. Pharmacies *(farmacias)* all display a green Maltese Cross.

Use adequate protection against the intense sun: wear a hat and apply factor 20-50 sun cream. Tap water in Tenerife is not drinkable but you can buy mineral water in big bottles in supermarkets.

There are A&E departments in Santa Cruz and and Playa de las Américas.

Santa Cruz de Tenerife: *Hospital Universitario Nuestra Señora de la Candelaria (Ctra Rosario 145 | tel. 922*

60 20 00); *Hospiten Rambla (La Rambla 115 | tel. 922 29 16 00 | hospiten.es)*.

Playa de las Américas/Los Cristianos: *Espacio de Salud DKV (Mon–Fri 8am–8pm | Av. Gómez Cuesta 22 | Playa de las Américas | tel. 922 10 22 02); Hospiten Sur (24hr service and hotel visits | C/ Siete Islas 8 | tel. 922 75 00 22 | hospiten.es)*.

Most doctors speak English but if you need complicated advice check online first.

ESSENTIALS

PUBLIC HOLIDAYS

1 Jan	Año Nuevo (New Year's Day)
6 Jan	Los Reyes (Epiphany)
March/April	Viernes Santo (Good Friday)
1 May	Día del Trabajo (Labour Day)
30 May	Día de las Islas Canarias (Canary Islands Day)
May/June	Corpus Christi
25 July	Santiago Apóstol (St James' Day)
15 Aug	Asunción (Assumption)
12 Oct	Columbus Day
1 Nov	Todos los Santos (All Saints' Day)
6 Dec	Constitution Day
8 Dec	Immaculate Conception
25 Dec	Christmas

BANKS

You can withdraw money at ATMs using your debit card. However, the fees are often exorbitant, so check in advance with your bank and find out where you will get the best rates and deals. Bank opening times vary but most are open Monday–Friday 8.30am–2pm and Saturdays 8.30am–1pm. Credit cards are accepted virtually everywhere.

BEACHES

The longest (3km) natural beach on the island is at El Médano in the southeast. The beaches between Los Cristianos and Costa Adeje in the south are artificial but very attractive. One of the most picturesque beaches (also artificial) is Playa de las Teresitas, north of Santa Cruz. The north is famous for its black beaches of which Playa del Jardín in Puerto de la Cruz is the nicest. Nudism is only allowed on a few beaches – for example, at Playa de la Tejita, west of El Médano; at Playa de Montaña Amarilla (Costa del Silencio); or at Playa de las Gaviotas, near Playa de las Teresitas.

CAMPING

The island has several campsites, e.g. *Camping-Caravaning Nauta (Cañada Blanca, Ctra 6225, Km1.5 | Las Galletas, Arona | tel. 922 78 51 18 | camping nauta.es/en); Camping El Castillo de Himeche (Guía de Isora | mobile tel. 6 86 25 89 54 | campingelcastillo dehimeche.com)* and *Camping Montaña Roja near El Médano (tel. 922 69 63 30 | monte.camp)*.

CUSTOMS

There are strict customs rules when flying home from the Canary Islands (even within the EU). Check these carefully, but you are normally limited to 200 cigarettes, 1 litre of spirits and 2 litres of wine.

LANGUAGE

In the larger resorts you will easily get by using English. However, a smattering of Spanish will come in very handy in more remote places or on public transport. See p. 144 for useful words and phrases

OPENING HOURS

Shops are usually open from 9/10am until 8pm. Many smaller shops will take a siesta (1.30–5pm). On Saturday most smaller places are only open until 2pm. Big supermarkets and shopping centres stay open 9am–9pm. Most restaurants serve food 1–4pm and 7–11pm and in holiday resorts from 12pm until well into the night.

PHONES

Spain's dialling code is 0034 after which you type in the nine-digit number (starting with the local dialling code 922). To call home, the UK is 0044, the US is 001 and Ireland is 01462 (then omit the first 0 of the number).

POST

You can buy stamps *(sellos)* at post offices *(correos)* and in newsagents *(estancos)*. Sending a letter *(carta)* or postcard *(tarjeta postal)* should cost between 1.50 euros and 2 euros. There are private postal services alongside the reliable national company – these may be cheaper but are not always reliable.

PRICES

The price you will have to pay for services (e.g. car repairs) is likely to be slightly higher than in the UK or in the US. Food costs about the same. Leisure and theme parks are especially expensive (easily 100 euros for a family of four). Food is generally cheap despite having to be imported and cigarettes and cosmetics are markedly cheaper than at home.

HOW MUCH DOES IT COST?

Coffee	*from 1.50 euros for a cup of coffee*
Food	*from 9 euros for a menú del día incl. a drink*
Petrol	*about 1.50 euros for 1 litre of unleaded*
Tapas	*from 3 euros for a tapa*
Taxis	*3.50 euros basic fare plus 1 euro/km*
Wine	*from 2 euros*

RURAL RETREATS

If you go on holiday to Tenerife, you don't have to stick to the coast. There are a number of agencies which rent out accommodation outside the major resorts, ranging from fincas that can sleep 10 people to a cave. They are normally pretty luxurious and prices are generally much lower than in hotels.

The main agency is *ATTUR (Asociación Tinerfeña de Turismo Rural | tel. 902 21 55 82 | webtenerife.co.uk). Turismo Rural (tel. 0405 60 44 88 | casasrurales.net | €€)* also has plenty of *Casas Rurales* (country houses) on its site.

TIPPING

If you are happy with service in a restaurant, round up the bill by about 10%. Hotel staff expect tips as do tour guides and taxi/coach drivers.

TOURIST INFORMATION

Tourist information is available at spain.info and from the following tourist offices:

LONDON

6th Floor, 64 North Row | London W1K 7DE | info.londres@tourspain.es
845 North Michigan Av., Suite 915-E |

CHICAGO

Chicago, IL 60611 | chicago@tourspain.es

LOS ANGELES

8383 Wilshire Blvd, Suite 956 | Beverly Hills, CA 90211 | losangeles@tourspain.es

NEW YORK

60 East 42nd St, Suite 5300 (53rd Floor) | New York, NY 10165-0039 | nuevayork@tourspain.es

TENERIFE

Arrivals hall of Reina Sofía Airport *(Mon–Fri 9am–9pm | Sat 9am–5pm | tel. 922 39 20 37)* and in all larger resorts on the island.

WEATHER IN TENERIFE

■ High season
■ Low season

	JAN	FEB	MARCH	APRIL	MAY	JUNE	JULY	AUG	SEPT	OCT	NOV	DEC
Daytime temperatures	21°	21°	22°	23°	24°	26°	28°	29°	28°	26°	23°	22°
Night-time temperatures	14°	14°	15°	16°	17°	19°	21°	21°	21°	19°	17°	16°
Hours of sunshine per day	5	6	7	8	10	11	11	11	9	7	5	5
Rainfall days per month	7	5	3	2	1	0	0	0	1	4	6	7
Water temperature in °C	19	18	18	18	19	20	21	22	23	23	21	20

☀ Hours of sunshine per day   ☂ Rainfall days per month   ≋ Water temperature in °C

WORDS & PHRASES
IN SPANISH

SMALLTALK

yes/no/maybe	**sí/no/quizás**
please Thank you	**por favor/gracias**
Hello!/Goodbye/Bye	**¡Hola!/¡Adiós!/¡Hasta luego!**
Good day/evening/night	**¡Buenos días!/¡Buenas tardes!/¡Buenas noches!**
Excuse me/sorry!	**¡Perdona!/¡Perdone!**
May I?	**¿Puedo …?**
Sorry?/Could you repeat?	**¿Cómo dice?**
My name is …	**Me llamo …**
What is your name? (formal/informal)	**¿Cómo se llama usted?/ ¿Cómo te llamas?**
I am from … the UK/USA/Ireland	**Soy de … Alemania/Austria/ Suiza**
I (don't) like this	**Esto (no) me gusta.**
I would like … /Do you have …?	**Querría …/¿Tiene usted …?**

SYMBOLS

EATING & DRINKING

The menu, please!	¡El menú, por favor!
expensive/cheap/price	caro/barato/precio
Could you bring ... please?	¿Podría traerme ... por favor?
bottle/jug/glass	botella/jarra/vaso
knife/fork/spoon	cuchillo/tenedor/cuchara
salt/pepper/sugar	sal/pimienta/azúcar
vinegar/oil/milk/lemon	vinagre/aceite/leche/limón
cold/too salty/undercooked	frío/demasiado salado/sin hacer
with/without ice/fizz (in water)	con/sin hielo/gas
vegetarian/allergy	vegetariano/vegetariana/alergía
I would like to pay, please	Querría pagar, por favor.
bill/receipt/tip	cuenta/recibo/propina

MISCELLANEOUS

Where is ...?/Where are ...?	¿Dónde está ...? /¿Dónde están ...?
What time is it?	¿Qué hora es?
today/tomorrow/yesterday	hoy/mañana/ayer
How much is ...?	¿Cuánto cuesta ...?
Where can I get internet/WiFi?	¿Dónde encuentro un acceso a internet/wifi?
Help!/Look out!/Be careful!	¡Socorro!/¡Atención!/¡Cuidado!
pharmacy/drug store	farmacia/droguería
broken/it's not working	roto/no funciona
broken down/garage	avería/taller
Can I take photos here?	¿Podría fotografiar aquí?
open/closed/opening hours	abierto/cerrado/horario
entrance/exit	entrada/salida
toilets (women/men)	aseos (señoras/caballeros)
(not) drinking water	agua (no) potable
breakfast/B&B/all inclusive	desayuno/media pensión/pensión completa
car park/multi-storey car park	parking/garaje
I would like to hire ...	Querría alquilar ...
a car/a bike/a boat	un coche/una bicicleta/un barco
0/1/2/3/4/5/6/7/8/9/10/100/1000	cero/un, uno, una/dos/tres/cuatro/cinco/seis/siete/ocho/nueve/diez/cien, ciento/mil

HOLIDAY VIBES
FOR RELAXATION & CHILLING

FOR BOOKWORMS & FILM BUFFS

🎥 ÓSCAR. THE COLOUR OF DESTINY (2008)
International co-production by Lucas Fernández about the life of the Canarian painter Óscar Domínguez, a contemporary and friend of Pablo Picasso. Many of his paintings are in the TEA in Santa Cruz.

🎥 CLASH OF THE TITANS (2009)
Who would have guessed that much of this Hollywood blockbuster starring Liam Neeson and Ralph Fiennes was filmed in Teide National Park.

🎥 JASON BOURNE (2016)
Paul Greengrass shot many scenes of the fifth installment of his *Bourne* film series (starring Matt Damon) in Tenerife. The island was chosen to illustrate places in Beirut, Athens and Reykjavík. The Plaza de España in Santa Cruz de Tenerife represented Syntagma Square in Athens.

📖 MORE KETCHUP THAN SALSA: CONFESSIONS OF A TENERIFE BARMAN (2005)
Joe Cawley's 2005 light-hearted look at life on the island from the viewpoint of a British expat.

PLAYLIST

0:58

‖ LOS SABANDEÑOS –
CANTATA DEL MENCEY LOCO
A traditional folk band singing mournfully about the "crazy Guanche rulers"

▶ GUERRILLA URBANA –
CANARIAS ES UNA ESTAFA
"The Canaries – a massive con". This is something of a recurring theme for this legendary La Laguna punk band

▶ ADEXE & NAU –
YO QUIERO VIVIR
Tenerife teens who have attracted millions of Youtube fans with their reggae

▶ ARISTIDES MORENO –
EL CAMBUYÓN
Caustic social commentary from an old Canarian crooner

▶ PEDRO GUERRA –
CONTAMINAME
Poetic singer-songwriter

The holiday soundtrack is available at **Spotify** under **MARCO POLO** Canaries

Or scan the code with the Spotify app

ONLINE

ILOVE ARONA 2.0
This app is a great way to get to know the south of the island, with details of fun whale-watching trips.

ARBOLAPP CANARIAS
Need help spotting dragos? This free app developed by various Spanish ministries allows you to identify trees on Tenerife.

RUTASTENERIFERURAL.COM
16 hiking routes (mainly in the north of Tenerife) with videos and maps.

ELCORAZONDETENERIFE.COM
"The heart of Tenerife" website comes with a free app and provides plenty of info on the capital and the Anaga mountains

STAR WALK
Enjoy the starry nights of Tenerife. The app can work out which way you are looking and tell you which stars you can see.

TRAVEL PURSUIT
THE MARCO POLO HOLIDAY QUIZ

Do you know what makes Tenerife tick? Test your knowledge of the idiosyncrasies and eccentricities of the island and its people. The answers are at the bottom of the page and can all be found on pages 18–23.

❶ Where did the first settlers of Tenerife come from?
a) From Europe
b) From America
c) From Africa

❷ What does the name "Guanche" mean?
a) Those who came from far away
b) The daughters of Tenerife
c) The sons of Tenerife

❸ The biggest festival on the island celebrates ...?
a) The Virgin Mary
b) The coming of Lent
c) The King of Spain

❹ What is a Canarian dragon *(drago)*?
a) A plant
b) An animal
c) A football mascot

❺ Who were the "Neveros"?
a) Nerve healers
b) The nine sons of the Guanche king
c) Ice cream vendors

❻ When was the last volcanic eruption on the island?
a) 1909
b) 3000 BCE
c) 1492

Answers: 1c, 2c, 3b, 4a, 5c, 6a, 7c, 8b, 9b, 10a, 11a, 12b

The celebrated Virgen de Candelaria

7 What is the name of Tenerife's crowned queen?
a) Reina Letizia
b) Reina Sofía
c) Virgen de Candelaria

8 What is the goal in Canarian wrestling?
a) To trap your opponent in a headlock
b) To skilfully bring your opponent to the floor
c) To achieve a knock-out any way you can

9 Where does most of the drinking water on the island come from?
a) It is brought over from the mainland on ships
b) It is obtained from the sea
c) It is extracted from clouds using a secret technique

10 How far is the European mainland (Spain's southern tip) from Tenerife?
a) More than 1,000km
b) Between 500 and 1,000km
c) Less than 500km

11 How high is Mount Teide, Spain's highest peak?
a) 3,718m
b) 2,001m
c) 1,500m

12 What is a Tenerife bugloss?
a) A type of local music
b) A bright red plant
c) A bright red cocktail

INDEX

WE WANT TO HEAR FROM YOU!

Did you have a great holiday? Is there something on your mind? Whatever it is, let us know! Whether you want to praise the guide, alert us to errors or give us a personal tip – MARCO POLO would be pleased to hear from you. Please contact us by email:

We do everything we can to provide the very latest information for your trip. Nevertheless, despite all of our authors' thorough research, errors can creep in. MARCO POLO does not accept any liability for this.

sales@heartwoodpublishing.co.uk

PICTURE CREDITS

Cover picture: Las Teresitas, Santa Cruz de Tenerife Shutterstock.com / Olena Tur
Photos: DuMont Bildarchiv: G. Hänel (139), M. Sasse (83); R. Freyer (52/53, 84/85); I. Gawin (92, 151); Getty Images/EyeEm: Korpics-Lukcs (105); R. Hackenberg (81); huber-images: A. Armellin (94/95), C. Dörr (20), O. Fantuz (113, 129), Mirau (62/63), A. Piai (30/31, 136/137), R. Schmid (6/7, 24/25, 26/27, 38/39, 46, 49, 57, 60, 75, 106, 109, 111, 124), F. Vallenari (66/67), R. Wittek (120/121), J. Wlodarczyk (2/3, 98/99); Laif: M. Gumm (73, 103), M. Sasse (8, 96, 115), Tophoven (58); Look: H. Erber (32/33), B. Merz (12/13, 86/87, 91); Look/age fotostock (back cover flap, 35); mauritius images/age fotostock (55, 79); mauritius images/AGF (148/149); mauritius images/Alamy: (9, 11, 14/15, 22, 45, 51, 116, 127), A. Polo (27); mauritius images/Cubolmages (76/77); mauritius images/imagebroker (front cover flap/1, 10, 118/119); vario images/Chromorange: W. G. Allgoewer (64); White Star: M. Gumm (28, 31, 146/147); E. Wrba (18)

4th Edition – fully revised and updated 2022
Worldwide Distribution: Heartwood Publishing Ltd, Bath, United Kingdom
www.heartwoodpublishing.co.uk

© MAIRDUMONT GmbH & Co. KG, Ostfilder
Authors: Izabella Gawin, Sven Weniger
Editor: Christin Ullmann
Picture editor: Anja Schlatterer

Cartography: © MAIRDUMONT, Ostfildern (pp. 36–37, 122, 126, 130, 135, outer wallet, fold-out map); Kompass Karten GmbH, A-Innsbruck © MAIRDUMONT, Ostfildern (p. 132); © MAIRDUMONT, Ostfildern, using mapping data under licence from OpenStreetMap, Lizenz CC-BY-SA 2.0 (pp. 36–37, 42–43, 68–69, 70, 88–89, 100–101, 104, 108).
Cover design and pull-out map cover design: bilekjaeger_Kreativagentur with Zukunftswerkstatt, Stuttgart
Page design: Langenstein Communication GmbH, Ludwigsburg

Heartwood Publishing credits:
Translated from the German by John Owen, Kathleen Becker, Jennifer Walcoff Neuheiser, Suzanne Kirkbright
Editors: Felicity Laughton, Kate Michell, Sophie Blacksell Jones
Prepress: Summerlane Books, Bath
Printed in India

MARCO POLO AUTHOR
IZABELLA GAWIN

Izabella only planned to spend one winter on the Canary Islands, but she felt so at home in the southern sun that she's been coming back every year – good-bye drizzle, farewell winter gloom! And because she found working on the Canaries as easy as living there, she ended up doing her PhD thesis on the islands and took to writing travel guides.

DOS & DON'TS

HOW TO AVOID SLIP-UPS & BLUNDERS

DON'T SWIM IF THERE'S A RED FLAG

Many people underestimate the strength of the current and overestimate their own swimming ability. If a red flag is flying at the beach, you must stay out of the water. Yellow means "be careful", and if the flag is green, you can jump right in.

DON'T CAUSE A BLOCKAGE

Lots of Canarian privies politely plead that paper should not be flushed down the loo. The pipes in older buildings here are very narrow and block easily so, if you're asked to, please put your paper in the bin!

DO BUY SEEDS

Calla lilies and mini dragon trees – some visitors can't help but dig up these indigenous plants to give them a new home in their gardens. However, Canarian plants are subject to special protection and they must not be removed from the islands. Instead, buy a packet of seeds in a flower shop (*jardinería*) – they are easier to pack too.

DO ASK BEFORE YOU BITE

Bread is part of every meal in Spain and once upon a time it was always free. Today it is often placed on your table … before appearing on your bill. It is a good idea to ask if it is *por cuenta de la casa* ("on the house").

DON'T WEAR FLIP-FLOPS IN THE MOUNTAINS

Tourists often start their trips in summery clothes on the coast only to be surprised by icy temperatures later on. The rule of thumb is: for every 100m in elevation, the temperature drops by 1°C. So, take a warm coat and suitable footwear.